UNIVERSITY OF NORTH CAROLINA
STUDIES IN THE ROMANCE LANGUAGES AND LITERATURES
Number 76

THE LAY OF GUINGAMOR:
A STUDY

THE LAY OF GUINGAMOR:
A STUDY

BY
SARA STURM

CHAPEL HILL
THE UNIVERSITY OF NORTH CAROLINA PRESS

TO HARLAN

DEPÓSITO LEGAL: V. 3.930-1968

ARTES GRÁFICAS SOLER, S. A. - JÁVEA, 30 - VALENCIA (8) - 1968

TABLE OF CONTENTS

	Pages
PREFACE	9
CHAPTER	
I. GUINGAMOR: A Fairy-Mistress Lay	11
II. GUINGAMOR: An Otherworld-Voyage Lay	44
III. GUINGAMOR: An Interpretation	79
BIBLIOGRAPHY	121

PREFACE

A knight, nephew of the king, refuses the queen's offer of love, then as a result of her veiled and vengeful challenge undertakes the pursuit of a famed white boar in a perilous forest from which none return. In the forest he encounters a fay who becomes his *amie*, and who alone can reward his hunt with success. After three joyful days spent in her company, which are in fact three hundred years, he insists upon returning to the court of his uncle to relate his *aventure* and to present the head of the boar, his token of success in the hunt. Forgetful of the fay's warning against partaking of food in the land of mortals, he eats three apples there. He is instantly overcome with age, and before the eyes of an astonished witness is carried away by two mysterious damsels, after which his story is commemorated in a lay.

Such is the story of the knight Guingamor, hero of the anonymous medieval lay which bears his name. Despite the literary merit of the poem, which led Gaston Paris to term it "le plus beau" of the group of anonymous lays which he published for the first time in 1879,[1] scholarly attention to it has taken primarily two directions: attempts to determine the position of the lay relative to the more famous poems of Marie de France, and studies of the motifs which it contains. The lay clearly presents the combination of two well-known traditions, of Fairy Mistress and of Otherworld Voyage; however, a study of the lay with respect to these traditions reveals a number of significant devia-

---

[1] G. Paris, "Lais inédits de Tyolet, de Guingamor, de Doon, du Lecheor et de Tydorel," *Romania*, VIII (1879), 29-79. All references to the text of *Guingamor* are to this edition.

tions from the typical patterns which they assume in medieval lay and romance. These deviations from pattern have generally been attributed to ineptitude on the part of the anonymous poet, who was, scholars have concluded, unable to fuse his story-types into a unified treatment.

The present study suggests that in fact the basic conception of the lay of *Guingamor* is neither of the two traditional motifs which form the complex narrative, the *matière* of the poem, but rather the presentation of a hero-quest in terms of Christian morality. In *Guingamor*, then, it is not the deviations from traditional patterns which require explanation, but rather the traditional elements which must be explained in terms of their contribution to this basic conception, the *sens* of the poem.

I should like to express my gratitude to Dr. Urban Tigner Holmes, Jr. of the University of North Carolina, whose sharing of his insight into medieval literature has been both generous and stimulating, and to Dr. Harry F. Williams of Florida State University, who introduced me to the study in depth of medieval literature and to the topic of the anonymous Breton lay. I should also like to thank the Research Foundation of the University of Kentucky for financial aid in preparing the manuscript of this study for publication.

Chapter I

GUINGAMOR: A FAIRY-MISTRESS LAY

The lay of Guingamor, like other lays and romances, presents the results of assimilation of a number of common motifs and narrative expedients. Among these the fairy element appears as the most characteristic, and the lay is usually classified in the fairy-mistress category. By its inclusion of this element, *Guingamor* resembles more or less closely a number of other medieval works, and in studying the poem itself it is important to determine the extent to which it directly represents a fairy-mistress tradition. This determination then becomes the necessary foundation for a more important study —that which distinguishes the poem from its medieval counterparts, determining its literary uniqueness.

The fairy-mistress tradition has deep roots and many branches, and critical opinion concerning the former especially is widely divergent. The various forms of the word "fairy" may be traced to the late Latin abstract noun *fatum*, "fate," [1] and there are a variety of supernatural beings in the folklore of many countries who correspond to J. A. MacCulloch's general definition: "Fairies are generally regarded as of a nature between spirits and men." [2] Scholars have tended to concentrate their search for the origins

---

[1] A number of other etymons have been suggested, from Greek, Hebrew, Anglo-Saxon, Persian, and Celtic. For enumeration and commentary by an author who accepts the Latin derivation, see T. Keightley, *The Fairy Mythology* (London, 1889), 4-13.

[2] "Fairy," in J. Hastings, ed., *Encyclopaedia of Religion and Ethics*, V (New York and Edinburgh, 1912), 679.

of the fay who plays so prominent a role in the *matière de Bretagne* in one of two directions, resulting in hypotheses of Celtic or of classic origins.

Lucy Paton in her *Studies in the Fairy Mythology of Arthurian Romance* asserts that the *fée* of lay and romance is a direct descendant of the Celtic fairy queen. If this conclusion is correct the roots of the *fée* are deep indeed, for according to Paton the typical Celtic fairy-mistress story "antedates at the latest the eighth century." [3] From three early Celtic tales —the *Imram Brain maic Febail* (*The Voyage of Bran, Son of Febal*), the *Echtra Condla* (*The Adventures of Connla*) and the story of *Pwyll, Prince of Dyved* from the *Mabinogion*— she attempts to construct a sort of prototype fairy queen, from whom the fay of Arthurian romance inherits her general characteristics: she is "essentially a supernatural woman, always more beautiful than the imagination can possibly fancy her, untouched by time, unhampered by lack of resources for the accomplishment of her pleasure, superior to human blemish, contingency, or necessity, in short altogether unlimited in her power." [4]

However, while the Arthurian fay shares these characteristics with her ancestress, she has undergone a long and complex evolution. Paton insists that to understand the true nature of the fay "we must follow her to her home in Ireland and Wales, where among the earlier traditions of the Celtic people she stands nearer simple myth than in many of the twelfth-century lays and romances." [5] This is no direct process, for those who assume the origin of the fay as we know her in the romance tradition to be Celtic have advanced a number of suggestions concerning what part of Celtic tradition she represents.

T. P. Cross stresses the importance of female water-divinities and water-names among the early Celts, [6] a fact which in his

---

[3] 2nd ed., with a survey of scholarship since 1903 and a bibliography by R. S. Loomis (New York, 1960), 248.

[4] *Ibid.*, pp. 4-5.

[5] *Ibid.*, p. 1.

[6] Paton points out that a number of interpretations proposed for the name of the fay Morgain have been connected with the sea. J. Rhys in his consideration of the Arthurian legend asserts that Morgain's name is the same as that of Morgen, the lady who in the *Vita Merlini* heals

opinion explains that the Arthurian hero often meets the *fée* by some body of water, particularly a fountain. In his view, several of the aspects of fay-mortal relationships are explained by a confusion between the Celtic water-*fée* and the swan-maiden of legend. Such a confusion or combination of characteristics was, he suggests, encouraged by the fact that early Celtic literature too has many Otherworld women appearing as birds, especially as swans. The two lays *Graelent* and *Guingamor*, in which the hero steals the clothes of a fay whom he finds bathing, in his opinion provide evidence for such a theory, for these clothes are best understood as "rationalized feather-skins" which, when captured, confer power over the fairy. [7] E. S. Hartland reports that in one type of swan-myth story the lady belongs to "a superior race to men, though properly in human form;" thus the swan-skin acquires "a distinct magical efficacy; so that when deprived of it, the maiden would be unable to effect the change," [8] and the man who could steal it would find her in his power. Eventually, the swan-story became rationalized to the extent that no allusion is made to either the shape-shifting of the maiden or the original feather-nature of the garment. [9]

Lucy Paton bases most of her conclusions concerning the fairy in Arthurian romance on a study of Morgain, the most notable of the fays named in the tradition. She rejects identifications of Morgain with water-spirits as based on name-forms rather than on roles. [10] Her choice as the ancestress of Morgain is the Morri-

---

Arthur's wounds (*Studies in the Arthurian Legend*, Oxford, 1891, p. 349); the name Morgen means, he says, "the offspring of the sea," and in its Irish form was the name "of a lake lady otherwise called Liban" (p. 7). Ferdinand Lot finds much more significant the Irish name Muirgen meaning "enfant de la mer," and contends that it was probably transmitted along with the belief in the Celtic Elysium, furnishing Geoffrey with his description of the *île fortunée* and with the name of the enchantress ("Nouveaux Essais sur la Provenance du Cycle Arthurien, II: La Passage des 'Lais Bretons'," *Romania*, XXVIII (1899), 1-48; discussed in Paton, pp. 10-11).

[7] "The Celtic Elements in the Lays of *Lanval* and *Graelent*," *MP*, XII, no. 10 (1915), 585-644.

[8] *The Science of Fairy Tales* (New York, 1891), 300.

[9] *Ibid.*, p. 301.

[10] "Except in so far as she is the inhabitant of an island, Avalon, she is never connected with the sea before the romance of *Floriant and Florete*,

gan, one of the five ancient Irish battle-goddesses, whose special function is "to incite to deeds of prowess and to plan battle" and who is frequently connected with the folk of the fairy hillocks, the Tuatha dé Danaan.[11]

R. S. Loomis proposed another Irish counterpart to Morgain. This is Macha, who like Lanval's mistress gave her hero wealth and a horse, imposed a taboo and punished its violation.[12] In another work he contends that Morgain's family relationships were patterned after those of Modron, who is in Welsh tradition the daughter of Avallach and wife of Urien, and in the *Mabinogion* the mother of Owain.[13] Thus it is apparent that for any characteristic of Morgain, however minor, the Celticists have a ready answer in the form of some Celtic prototype, be she a mermaid, a battle-goddess, or the descendant of a Gallo-Roman goddess in turn.[14]

E. Faral presents the case for classic derivation.[15] Like Rhŷs and Lot, he attempts to determine the origin of the name Morgen which makes its first appearance in the *Vita Merlini*. We find that she is in that work the eldest and most beautiful of nine sisters who reign in the isle of Avalon, is presented as a great healer, is capable of metamorphoses, and can fly.[16] Most of these elements are borrowed, according to Faral, from ancient authors' accounts of certain famous isles.[17] Thus only the names of Morgen

---

a late source, where her association with the water is probably due to the influence of local tradition in Sicily" (*op. cit.*, pp. 10-11).

[11] *Ibid.*, p. 11. For a summary of Paton's conclusions concerning Morgain, see pp. 162-66. Aware that not all the Arthurian fays are clearly explicable by reference to Morgain, Paton discusses also the Dame du Lac and Niniane. For her summary of the role of the three fays and their development in Arthurian romance, see pp. 248-49.

[12] "A Survey of Scholarship on the Fairy Mythology of Arthurian Romance since 1903," in Paton, *op. cit.*, 2nd ed. (New York, 1960), 283-4.

[13] *Celtic Myth and Arthurian Romance* (New York, 1927), 192.

[14] Celtic scholars agree, says Loomis, that Modron is the old Gallo-Roman goddess Matrona who gave her name to the Marne and was associated with the waters (*ibid.*, p. 193).

[15] "L'Ile d'Avallon et la Fée Morgan," in *Mélanges Jeanroy* (Paris, 1928), 243-53.

[16] *Ibid.*, pp. 246-47.

[17] That of the island's fecundity is found in Isidore's description of the Canaries (*Etymologiae* XIV, 6, 8), that of the longevity enjoyed there from Solinus, *Collectanea rerum memorabilium*, LIV, 11, concerning the

and her eight sisters may be considered new to Geoffrey, and these names he probably invented without recourse to any "tradition galloise qu'il avait recueillie parmi ses contemporains." [18]

These, then, are the major hypothetical roots of the Arthurian fairy tradition. The branches of that tradition, while richly varied, have not been subject to so much dispute. The study of those branches is the study of the role, or roles, which the fay assumes in lay and romance.

This "supernatural woman" has a major role in the Arthurian tales, as in the older Celtic tales from which she may derive, because of her relation to a man. This man is not supernatural; nor is he, like the fay, immortal. However, although he remains subject to "human necessity," he is never an ordinary mortal. Paton notes of the fairy that insistent love is a fundamental part of the fay's nature, but that she "holds aloof from ordinary mortals and gives her favor only to the best and most valorous of knights." [19]

The relation of the fay to her chosen knight-hero assumes a pattern —or rather, one of a number of variants on a basic pattern— in the lay and romance material. It is the fairy who chooses the knight, and has in some versions even protected him from infancy. At the appropriate time, often at some period of crisis in the hero's life, she summons him to the Otherworld. This call may come as a complete surprise to the hero, or he may even fail to recognize it as such, but it is always part of the fairy's careful plan. The hero has no choice; willingly or no, he obeys the summons of the fay. As a result he becomes a resident

---

Isle of Taprobane; the nine ladies and their healing powers are found in Pomponius Mela's account of the Isle of Sein, *De Situ orbis*, III, 16 (*ibid.*, pp. 247-49). E. K. Chambers too is of the opinion that Geoffrey may owe this detail to "a specific Breton belief" recorded most fully by Pomponius Mela, "that the island of Sena off the coast of Gaul was the home of nine virgin priestesses, shape-shifters, controllers of the sea and winds by their spells, and skilled alike in medicine and divination" (*Arthur of Britain*, London, 1927, p. 219).

[18] Geoffrey, who was no doubt familiar with the classic poets' frequent reference to the Muses as the nine sisters, knew also that each of these Muses had a name; to make them true "fées de Bretagne," he naturally named them *à la bretonne* (*ibid.*, pp. 251-52).

[19] *Op. cit.*, p. 5.

of the Otherworld, where his life is one of constant delight. After an indeterminate period, either due to his own longing to return to his land or because of the fay's decisions as to when and where he may enjoy her company, he is separated from his mistress; however, he is not entirely detached from her, as upon his return to the mortal world she gives him some sort of command. In the typical tale, he forgets the command or is for some reason unable to obey it, and the serious consequences predicted by the fairy inevitably follow, threatening him with disgrace or even death. Also typically, the fairy returns at the last moment, rescuing the penitent hero. She then carries him away, and he is presumed to be restored to favor and to live with her "forever after."

The fairy's choice of the knight appears in the earliest of the known Celtic tales involving a supernatural creature's love for a mortal. For example, in the *Echtra Condla* as summarized by Paton, the hero was standing with his father when he saw a strange and beautiful woman. "She was visible only to Connla, and for him alone had she come to tell him that she loved him and to summon him to her dwelling in the lands of the living, where neither death nor sin were known, and where Connla's youth would never wither, a land that was justly called the Plain of Delight." Similarly, a lady on a snow-white horse tempts the hero Pwyll to pursue her, and explains to him that "she was journeying on her own errand... and her chief quest was to seek him. She was Rhiannon, she said, the daughter of Heveydo Hên, who wished to give her to a husband against her will; but such was her love for Pwyll that him alone would she have for a husband." [20]

This sort of episode is repeated in the later lays and romances, as illustrated by the way in which Lanval makes the acquaintance of his beautiful *amie*. Lying in a meadow, he sees two beautiful damsels approaching, and as he rises to meet them they greet him at once:

> 'Sire Lanval, ma dameisele,
> Que tant est pruz e sage e bele,

---

[20] *Ibid.*, pp. 3-4.

Ele nus enveie pur vus;
Kar i venez ensemble od nus!' (vv. 71-74)

He immediately and unquestionningly follows them, and Marie is no doubt paying tribute to the fabled irresistible power of the fairy's call when she adds that "De sun cheval ne tient nul plait, Que devant lui pesseit al pre" (vv. 78-79). Lanval sits beside the lady who had summoned him to her tent, and she explains her presence:

'Lanval,' fet ele, 'beus amis,
Pur vos vienc jeo fors de ma tere;
De luinz vus sui venu(e) quere...' (vv. 110-12)

Following the choice of the hero is the so-called induction, on which there are a number of variations. It relates the actual entry of the mortal into the Otherworld. The hero is drawn to the fairy irresistibly; as Paton points out, "her power is at first manifested by some mysterious agency." This characteristic is found already in the early Celtic tales: Bran listens to a musical bough which numbs the senses; Connla is given a magic apple which, while it never grows smaller as he eats of it each day, increases his longing for the fairy; Rhiannon rides by Pwyll on a snow-white horse which only the hero can catch. "The effect of these agencies is merely the sign that the mortal is feeling the bewildering fairy influence, and unconsciously, but perforce, yielding to it." [21]

In the later lays and romances, the fairy may manifest her power in any number of ways, but two are common: the hunt and the magic boat. In the hunt sequence her technique involves "sending out a fairy messenger disguised as some tempting victim for the huntsman's dart, usually a stag, a boar, or a bird, which lures the young knight to her domain." [22] Examples are numerous. As R. S. Loomis points out, in the *Manawydan* of the *Mabinogi* Pryderi pursued a pure white boar into an enchanted castle, where it disappeared; [23] Graelent, Guigemar, Guingamor all are engaged

---

[21] *Ibid.*, p. 5.
[22] *Ibid.*, p. 15.
[23] *Arthurian Tradition and Chrétien de Troyes* (New York, 1949), 69.

in hunting some elusive and enticing prey when they reach the boundary of the Otherworld.

The situation in *Guigemar* is particularly interesting in this regard, as the actual role of the fairy in the story is not quite clear, Marie having reduced the supernatural aspects in order perhaps to emphasize the 'roman d'amour.' The white hind wounded by Guigemar, suggests Ewert, is in fact a fairy; "but the mission of the fairy is not revealed too clearly and we are left free to imagine her (as Hoepffner does) metamorphosed in Marie's version into the 'mal mariée' with whom the hero falls in love, were it not that the fairy's own predictions give no hint of this and there is nothing supernatural about the lady... save that she is able to leave the castle despite bolts and bars." [24]

The equally common device of the magic boat is frequently found in conjunction with the hunt. After Guigemar wounds the hind and is himself wounded, he enters a magic ship which bears him away; the fairy Melior, in *Partonopeus de Blois*, sends a magic ship for the hero, who has been lost from his companions during the course of a boar-hunt; in the prose *Tristan*, the mysterious *Nef de Joie*, a creation of Merlin, carries the hero with Iseut to Logres. Connla in the Celtic story previously mentioned accompanies the fairy to the Plain of Delight in her marvellous glass ship; Perceval has a similar mysterious voyage. [25] The essential element in these two types of induction is that in both, the fairy has deliberately arranged either the hunt, or the magic boat, or the two together as a means of conveying the hero to the Otherworld.

The nature of the hero's residency in the Otherworld varies somewhat with the nature of that Otherworld as conceived by the author of a given work, a point to be considered in the following chapter. One of the major variants is its location. In the *Lanval* episode the knight is never physically transported to another place to enjoy the company of his *amie*; rather, she appears to him whenever he wishes, bringing with her all the mysterious powers of fairyland. More common, however, is the actual voyage of

---

[24] A. Ewert, ed., *Marie de France, Lais* (Oxford, 1944), 165.
[25] See Paton, p. 16, n. 1 for further examples.

the hero-mortal to the Otherworld, which may be located under the waters, in the sky, or in some mysterious place on the earth itself, in every case surrounded by some line of demarkation which separates it from the ordinary world.

During his stay in the Otherworld, the hero enjoys a life of luxury and delight. Food and drink are exquisite and plentiful. Companionship is never lacking, both that of his *amie* and, often, that of other favored knights each of whom has his own fair companion. The richness and beauty of clothing, vessels, and other objects are frequently described at length; the place of residence itself may be presented as a magnificent castle, constructed of gold, silver, and precious stones. Time passes in the pursuit of pleasure, often in games such as chess; frequently the air is filled with music.

This aspect of the residence of the hero in fairyland is one of the least variable elements of the fairy-mistress tale. There are, in addition, tales of a similar type in which the hero's enjoyment of such delights is contingent upon his accomplishment of certain exploits specified by the fay. The fay who makes such demands upon her chosen hero belongs, according to Alfred Nutt, to a type of being who "appears... in every form and at all periods of Celtic mythic literature, and forms one of the most distinctive and characteristic personages of that literature," the supernatural woman "who instructs a young hero in the manly exploits —skill in arms or the chase— that fit him for some special purpose." [26]

Paton cites as illustrations of this type of fairy-to-hero relationship the lay of *Tyolet* and Renaud de Beaujeu's *Bel Inconnu*. Tyolet's first adventure, which results in his becoming king of the land of Logres, is set by a beautiful maiden who promises herself in marriage to the knight who can cut off the white foot of a shining stag which is guarded by seven lions. The hero, guided to the stag by the maiden's brachet, charms it by means of a magical gift of whistling taught him in his youth by a fay:

> Une fée ci li ora,
> Et a sifler li enseigna:

---

[26] In *Folk Lore Record*, IV (1881), 32; quoted in Paton, p. 170.

>   Dex onc nule beste ne fist
>   Qu'il a son sifler ne preist. (vv. 45-48)

He is thus enabled to cut off the stag's foot, and after demonstrating his prowess by killing the lion he is granted the maiden's love and becomes king in her land. The early episodes tinged with magic in Tyolet's life are thus "the means employed by the fay to prepare him for his final quest, and to compel him to the series of adventures that will give him to her for her lord."[27] This Otherworld influence has thus been his constant guide.

A second example of the type, and one which shows an interesting modification of the pattern, is the *Biaus Desconeüs*. The fay who guides Guinglain's progress in knighthood is the maiden of the Ile d'Or, *la pucele as blances mains*. After the hero accomplishes his quest to rescue Blonde Esmerée from a spell, a mysterious voice tells Guinglain his name, and that he is the son of the fay Blanchemal and of Gawain. Having deserted the Ile d'Or maiden to complete his quest, he now longs to return to her; with great difficulty he wins her favor again, and learns that she has been the guiding force in his knightly adventures. She it was who had loved him from his youth and aided him throughout his career, even influencing Blonde Esmerée's messenger to go to Arthur's court with her appeal to which Guinglain was certain to respond. It was also she who told him his name when his quest was completed.

>   Sacie molt me sui entremisse
>   En tos sanblans, en tos servisse,
>   Coment avoir je vos peüsse
>   Ne coment vostre amie fusse
>   Or vos ai je, Dius en ait los! (vv. 5005-09)

Returning to the hero of the basic fairy-mistress tale, whom we left enjoying the delights of the Otherworld, we find that after an indefinite period he is separated from his *amie*. Frequently this separation is due to his insistence on returning to his home, for which he feels great nostalgia. The fairy in this case is generally opposed to the return, and frequently warns

---

[27] *Op. cit.*, p. 172.

him that he will suffer if he insists. In the Irish story of Bran, the hero and his comrades dwelt in the Otherworld for many years, but eventually one of them was seized with homesickness, and persuaded Bran to return with him to Ireland. "The woman said to them that their going would make them rue. However, they went, and the woman said that none of them should touch the land." But the man who had yielded to the pangs of homesickness leaped out of their vessel; "as soon as he touched the earth of Ireland, forthwith he was a heap of ashes, as though he had been in the earth for many hundred years." [28]

In *Lanval* the fairy's commandment to the knight is of a different nature, consistent with Marie's general treatment of the story. The fairy-mistress type is already transformed by Marie in the fact that Lanval is not taken away to the Otherworld by his *amie*, and here his separation from her is actually caused, not by his decision, but by hers. At evening she sends him away:

> 'Amis,' fet ele, 'levez sus!
> Vus n'i poëz demurer plus.
> Alez vus en, jeo remeindrai...' (vv. 159-61)

but has first made him promise never to tell of their love:

> 'Ami,' fet ele, 'or vus chasti,
> Si vus comant e si vus pri,
> Ne vus descovrez a nul humme!
> De ceo vus dirai ja la summe:
> A tuz jurs m'avriez perdue,
> Se ceste amur esteit seüe...' (vv. 143-48)

This commandment differs from the type of fairy injunction found in *Bran* and many other tales in that it threatens, not harm or death to the hero if he breaks it, but rather the loss of the fay's love.

The commandment to avoid mention of the fay has been studied by Hartland as a taboo, defining the term in the folklore sense of "any injunction addressed by a supernatural being to the

---

[28] *The Voyage of Bran*, ed. Kuno Meyer (London, 1895), I, 32.

hero or heroine of a tale." [29] Taboo is in its original impulse an "interminable penetration of the religious sanction into all reaches of human activity," and thus a matter of the most serious concern. [30] The specific injunction to secrecy is traced by Hartland to the fear of savage peoples at the utterance of their names, a fear whose origin "seems to have been the dread of sorcery," the superstition that knowledge of one's name conferred power over one. [31] T. P. Cross, too, mentions the prevalence in Celtic tales of this taboo, noting that supernatural beings shrink from publicity. [32] Ewert describes the specific injunction to secrecy as a commonplace of fairy tales, and ties Marie's use of it to contemporary theories of love —"one of whose chief tenets was the obligation of the lover to observe the utmost discretion." [33]

The circumstances under which the hero breaks the fairy's commandment also vary. Like Bran's companion, the hero may be so eager upon returning to his homeland that he forgets the warning not to set foot on the land or to touch some taboo object. In the Irish legend of *Oisin*, which bears a number of resemblances to Guingamor, the hero desires to return to Erin to see his father. His fairy-wife protests: "If you must go to Erin, I'll give you this white steed to carry you; but if you come down from the steed or touch the soil of Erin with your foot, the steed will come back that minute, and you'll be where he left you, a poor old man..." Oisin hastens to return to Erin, and under a stone he finds the great horn used to call the Fenians to assemble. The herdsman whom he meets there refuses to attempt to bring the horn to him; "with that Oisin moved near the horn, and reaching down took it in his hand; but so eager was he to blow it that he forgot everything, and slipped in reaching till one foot touched the earth. In an instant the steed was gone, and Oisin lay on the ground a blind old man." [34] In a literary form of the theme,

---

[29] *Op. cit.*, p. 270.

[30] J. R. Reinhard, *The Survival of Geis in Medieval Romance* (Halle, 1933), 12. Reinhard's introduction is a detailed presentation of geis as a form of taboo.

[31] *Op. cit.*, p. 309.

[32] *Op. cit.*, p. 622.

[33] *Op. cit.*, p. 173.

[34] J. Curtin, *Myths and Folk-Lore of Ireland* (Boston, 1890), 332-33.

the *Lay of Oisin in the Land of Youth*, he disobeys the same command, with the same results.[35]

Lanval's case is again more subtle. The queen, angered by the knight's rejection of her unwelcome advances, insults him. Yielding to the extreme provocation, Lanval

> Del respundre ne fu pas lent.
> Teu chose dist par maltalent
> Dunt il se repenti sovent. (vv. 288-90)

He breaks the fairy's commandment by replying not only that he has an *amie*, but that she is much more fair than the queen.

The residence of the hero in the Otherworld is sometimes referred to as a "fairy retention."[36] This appellation is quite accurate in many episodes of medieval romance, but it is essential to differentiate such episodes from the basic fairy-mistress tale with which they are sometimes confused. In this type of fairy-loves-hero story, the fay may lure the hero to the Otherworld by the methods previously noted, or she may use stronger methods such as drugging him or inducing in him a deep sleep. In the Otherworld, the hero either refuses at once to give his love to the fay, or succumbs to her charms for some time but eventually rejects her, determining to return to his own people, perhaps to his wife or to a mortal *amie*. The fairy, thus spurned, reacts with indignation or with rage, and vengefully becomes his enemy. Paton lists a number of tales of this type, among them the Renoart story in the *Bataille Loquifer*, the prose *Lancelot*, and the adventures of Alisander l'Orphelin.[37] Many *aventures* in the romances concerning the temporary captivity of knights by fairies in enchanted castles reflect this same sort of relationship. Here, says Paton, "the fairy retention has become a serious imprisonment behind iron bars; the hero's escape can no longer be accomplished by the permission of the fay coupled with an injunction."[38] In this type of tale, a fairy spurned is dangerous; she seeks to

---

[35] A. Nutt, "The Happy Otherworld in the Mythico-Romantic Literature of the Irish," in *The Voyage of Bran*, ed. Meyer, p. 151.
[36] Paton, p. 54.
[37] *Ibid.*, pp. 49-59.
[38] *Ibid.*, p. 54.

detain the hero in the Otherworld, often against his wishes, for her own purposes, frequently actually to do him harm.[39]

There is no doubt that in this type of story the hero's stay in the Otherworld may be termed an imprisonment; but whether his residence there in the basic fairy-mistress type of tale may correctly be termed a "retention" is open to question. To use such a term is to assume that during his stay in the Otherworld the hero's will is constantly under the influence of the fairy spell, and that without that influence he would not choose to remain. Although the fairy's power of "putting a spell upon mortals which holds them bound for a long period of time" is unquestioned, there is considerable evidence in the tales to indicate that such spells are not always necessary —that, on the contrary, the hero who is chosen by the fairy to live with her in the Otherworld is considered fortunate. Since the fairies are presented as supernaturally beautiful and desirable creatures, it is perhaps an over-emphasis of the fairy's magical powers to assume that their constant exercise was always necessary in order to detain the hero in a place where he experienced only delight.

It is possible to conceive of a simple explanation for the diverging fairy traditions, by noting what they indisputably share. We find that the fairy-mistress and the fairy-retention types of tales have in common two elements. In the first place, the fay is, on her own initiative, seeking out a mortal hero

---

[39] Paton attempts to establish a common derivation for the basic type of fairy-mistress tale and that involving a captivity, a derivation to be found in the ancestry of the fay Morgain as traced to the Irish war-goddess the Morrigan. Morgan figures in the romance material as both a typical fairy mistress and an unscrupulous, willful fay, and the prototype of the latter role may be found in the story of her hostility to Arthur. The variations in the role assigned to Morgain are in Paton's opinion explained by the hypothesis that in them the fierce character of the Morrigan is evident to a greater or lesser extent; "for the nature of the war-goddess was slow to die even when its representative had by tradition most nearly merged into the proud, unscrupulous lady of a medieval castle" (*op. cit.*, p. 72). J. Rhys asserts that the varying characteristics of the fay "may all be taken as different aspects of the one mythic figure, the lake lady Morgen" (*Studies*, p. 348) and, later, that a distinction is necessary. The romances, he says, "spoke of a lake lady Morgain, Morgan, or Morgue. The character varied: Morgain le Fay was a designing or wicked person, but Morgan was also the name of a well-disposed lady of the same fairy kind (*Celtic Folklore, Welsh and Manx*, Oxford, 1901, 374).

of her own choosing, whom she desires as her lover. Secondly, she relates to him through the use of her magical powers. It is not difficult to see the appeal to man's imagination of the fairy-mortal relationship. A race of creatures between spirits and men, with magical powers which make them superior to men, and who, furthermore, far surpass human beauty; creatures who nonetheless so desire the love of mortal men that they want nothing more than to extend to their chosen heroes all the delights of the Otherworld —such is the stuff that the fairy romances are made of. Whether the fairy be a benevolent mistress or, rebuffed, a willful and malevolent captor, the fascination of the relationship between fairy woman and mortal man whom she desires is the interest-nucleus of the tale.

What, then, of *Guingamor* as a fairy-mistress lay? In terms of the usual classifications proposed for the lays, it is certainly to the fairy-mistress group that *Guingamor* belongs, and analysis reveals that in a number of ways the poem follows the typical pattern. But it also departs from that pattern in a number of particulars, as do many other fairy-mistress stories, and a number of problems of interpretation arise for which consideration of the work as a fairy-mistress lay does not seem to provide answers.

The first element of the typical fairy-mistress tale involves the fairy's choice of the hero and her summons to him. No fairy comes to seek Guingamor. Neither is there a fairy messenger, nor any sort of mysterious call which may be readily identified as such. There is, however, a boar, and we recall that the fairy's technique may involve "sending out a fairy messenger disguised as some tempting victim for the huntsman's dart, usually a stag, a boar, or a bird, which lures the young knight to her domain." [40] Guingamor does in fact eventually encounter the fay while in pursuit of the boar, but the circumstances of the pursuit must be examined.

Guingamor does not come upon the mysterious boar suddenly while hunting or wandering in the forest. He enters the forest specifically to pursue the boar, and not because it is a "tempting victim." This latter point is significant: he is not drawn irresis-

---

[40] Paton, p. 15.

tibly by any fairy spell, or by any force which might be so interpreted. Rather, there are very precise reasons for his undertaking the hunt, and these have no apparent connection with the fairy. The fundamental reason is that the queen has offered him her love, and he has refused it.

This offer and refusal present the well-known Potiphar's-wife motif. The story of a high-born lady who offers her love to a young man and, when it is refused, seeks to bring him harm, is very widespread. Rhŷs states that Irish mythology, in order to account for the Mórrígu or Great Queen's antagonism to the hero Cúchulinn, explained that "she had, in a weak moment, made love to him, and that he had given her a rebuff which she keenly resented." [41] Schofield notes some interesting versions. In the *Hjalmters og Olvers Saga* the hero roughly refuses the advances of his step-mother, who seeks revenge, and in the following chapter "the hero vainly pursues a hind into a forest, which leads him to a giant's cave. This is evidently a result of the step-mother's machinations." [42] In another article Schofield points out the resemblance to episodes in the *Dolopathos* and the *Seven Sages*: in both "the only excuse given for the narration of the collection of stories" is that "the wife of the king plotted secretly to rid herself of the young heir to the throne, by whom she had been indignantly repulsed when she offered to become his *amie*." [43] The popular ballad "The Queen of Scotland" recorded by Child tells of the Queen's invitation to young Troy Muir to share her bed:

> 'O God forbid,' this youth then said
> 'That ever I drie sic blame
> As ever to touch the queen's bodie
> Altho the king's frae hame.'
> When that he had these words spoken,
> She secretly did say,

---

[41] *Studies*, p. 228.

[42] The espisode is found in the *Fornmanna Sögur*, III, 469ff.; quoted in W. H. Schofield, "The Lays of Graelent and Lanval and the Story of Wayland," *PMLA*, XV (1900), 147.

[43] "The Lay of Guingamor," (*Harvard*) *Studies and Notes in Philology and Literature*, V (1896), 233.

> 'Some evil I shall work this man,
> Before that it be day.' [44]

In the romance material the motif occurs, for example, in the well-known story of the *Chatelaine de Vergi;* more importantly for our present study, it is found in the two fairy-mistress lays whose similarities to *Guingamor* are often noted: *Lanval* and *Graelent*. In each of these the offended queen chooses a different means to bring harm to the man by whom she has been rejected. In *Lanval* she complains to the king of the knight's unflattering remarks; in *Graelent* she influences the king to withhold from his loyal knight any reward for service. The queen's mention of the dangerous *aventure* in *Guingamor*, then, may appear as merely an unusually ingenious and subtle device to rid herself of a knight whose presence has become intolerable.

There are, however, significant differences between the development of the motif in *Guingamor* and that commonly found in such tales, differences which appear when the relation of the incident to the rest of the tale is considered. In *Lanval* the knight's offending comments to the queen follow his encounter with the fay, and are based in part on his existing relationship with his *amie*. In *Graelent*, which in this respect provides a closer parallel to *Guingamor*, the hero leaves the court saddened by the results of the queen's influence after his rejection of her, and wanders into the forest where he spies a white hart; the animal soon leads him to the waiting fay. In *Guingamor* the connection between the rebuff to the queen and the encounter with the fay is much more tenuous. Eager to be rid of the knight who has refused her, the queen mentions to the assembled knights the mysterious boar:

> 'Molt vos oi,' fet ele, 'vanter,
> Et vos aventures conter.
> Mes n'a ceanz nul si hardi,
> De toz iceus que je voi ci,
> Qui en la forest ci defors,
> La ou converse li blans pors,
> Osast chacier ne soner cor,

---

[44] Ballad no. 301; quoted in Schofield, "Graelent and Lanval," p. 147.

> Qui li donroit mil livres d'or.
> En merveilleus los le metroit,
> Qui le sengler prendre porroit.' (vv. 153-162)

Guingamor knows at once, in the ensuing silence, that the queen has set a trap for him with these words, "Qu'elle a por lui cest plet meu" (v. 166). We learn of the extreme danger of the hunt, which the king calls "l'aventure de la forest" (v. 171); for

> Onques nus hom n'i pot aler
> Qui puis em peust reperier,
> Por qoi le porc peust chacier... (vv. 174-76)

In fact, the ten best knights known to the king have attempted the hunt, and all have been lost. Guingamor, however, for reasons which are not immediately clear, is at once determined to undertake this *aventure,* and even the king is unable to dissuade him.

This introductory episode of the lay has puzzled scholars. Schofield in his careful study states that "we see at once that it has no inherent connection with the rest of the poem. It is evident that this story of the depravity of the wife in high station was originally extraneous to our account."[45] Segre, in whose opinion *Guingamor* compares unfavorably with *Graelent* and *Lanval,* considers the means of revenge chosen by the queen to be a major weakness in the poem: "Si ricorderà che in *Graelent* la regina delusa riesce a far diminuire dal re gli appannaggi di Graelent, così da ridurlo in povertà e da impedirgli di cercarsi un altro signore: l'autore di *Guingamor* deve avere ritenuto, e giustamente, poco brillante questa soluzione narrativa, ma l'a sostituita con una non migliore."[46] The question of the function of this introductory episode will be considered in the final chapter of this study.

It is at least apparent that when Guingamor enters the forest to pursue the boar, no discernable fairy influence is responsible. Some scholars, however, have not been deterred by this absence of evidence that the boar is fairy-related. H. Newstead, for exam-

---

[45] "Guingamor," p. 237.
[46] C. Segre, "Lanval, Graëlent, Guingamor," *Studi in onore di Angelo Monteverdi,* II (Modena, 1959), 761.

ple, assumes that the hunt in *Guingamor*, like that in *Partonopeus*, "was instigated by a fay."[47] Lot asserts a resemblance between *Graelent* and *Guingamor* in this respect, referring to the fay encountered by Guingamor as "la pucelle qui entraîne le héros dans un autre monde."[48] Newstead compares *Graelent* to *Guingamor*: "Just as Guingamor hunts a white fairy boar, so Graelent pursues a snow-white hind," the significance of both animals being that they lead to the encounter with the fay and are sent for that purpose,[49] and Reinhard too includes *Guingamor* among a number of tales in which "the chase, of whatsoever animal, seems to have been arranged, somehow, by the fairy in order to bring about the meeting with the hero."[50] But while it is true that in *Graelent* the white hart is no doubt one of the type of "fairy messengers" sent to "tempt the huntsman's dart," in *Guingamor* the author has been very careful to show that his hero enters the forest for very specific, this-world reasons. Whether, in so doing, the author destroyed the coherence of the tale —as Schofield and Segre would maintain— is a question which must be delayed; for the present it is important to observe that in *Guingamor*, in contrast to *Graelent* and to *Lanval*, the fairy element is effectively eliminated from the first section of the lay.

Guingamor's entry into the forest should, according to the fairy-mistress pattern, correspond to the beginning of the induction episode, and his pursuit of the boar should be merely the means by which he is led to the fairy. In the poem, however, the hunt itself is described at great length —almost 100 lines, of a total of 678— and in great detail. The various manoeuvres of the boar, the brachet, and the hunter are all presented. Guingamor loses sight of the boar, finds it again, and in following it at great speed suddenly finds himself before "un grant palès" (v. 365). Entering on horseback, he marvels at its splendor; it is entirely uninhabited. Suddenly he realizes that he has lost both the boar and the very valuable brachet of his uncle the king. Greatly

---

[47] "The Traditional Background of *Partonopeus de Blois*," *PMLA*, LXI (1946), 931.

[48] F. Lot, "Nouveaux Essais sur la Provenance du Cycle Arthurien, III," *Romania*, XXVIII (1899), 327.

[49] "Partonopeus," p. 925.

[50] *Op. cit.*, p. 281.

alarmed, he listens for any indication of their direction, and finally hears both the dog and the quarry. He sounds his horn and rides in the direction of the cries, but "li pors s'en est outre passez" (v. 418). Reaching "el chief de la lande," he finds a lovely fountain, and in it "une pucele s'i baingnoit" —the fay, making her appearance after 426 lines of a lay which has a total of 678.

Guingamor's original encounter with the fay has been the subject of scholarly speculation. Schofield, among others, has pointed out the traditional nature of the fairy in the fountain, and the very close parallel between the account in *Guingamor* and that in *Graelent*. The water of the fountain is *clere et bele* (*Graelent* 209; *Guingamor* 425); the *pucele* who is bathing there has two attendants in *Graelent*, one in *Guingamor*. In both accounts she is *despoulie* of her clothes, which are seen nearby, and in both the knight takes the clothes to keep the fay from leaving.[51] Schofield's examination of this episode of the capture of the maiden bathing, which is in his opinion "the climax of the introduction and the object of all that precedes," is based on a comparison of the similar versions in *Graelent* and *Guingamor* to the *Dolopathos*, which in turn leads him to the Latin prose *Dolopathos* of Johannes de Alta Silva on which Herbert's French tale was patterned; for "this story which so closely resembles a part of *Guingamor* is an early and truly popular version of the swan-maiden story introduced by John of Alta Silva into the Oriental setting of the Seven Sages from popular tradition."[52]

The Latin account of the capture of the maiden is as follows: "Fontem repperit nymphamque in eo virginem cathenam auream tenentem manu, nudaque membra lavantem conspicit. Cuius statim pulchritudine et amore captus, illa non presciente accurrit, cathenamque, in qua virtus et operatio virginis constabat, aufferens, ipsam nudam inter bracchia de fonte repente levat." This golden chain contained her power, and corresponds to the original feather-garment of the swan-maiden. Deprived of it, she cannot leave her human form, and the hero's capture of the chain is thus the capture of the maiden. Herbert in the French version of the *Dolopathos* is quite specific about the power of the chain:

---

[51] "Guingamor," pp. 228-29.
[52] *Ibid.*, pp. 234-35.

> En la chaaigne fut sans doute
> Sa vertu et sa force toute:
> N'ot pooir de soi desfandre.

The authors of *Graelent* and *Guingamor*, aware of the resemblance of the genuine fountain-fay in their stories to the swan-maiden type of heroine just described, were unable to keep the two separate, Schofield suggests, with the result that the hero captures the garments of the maiden whom he finds bathing; but "to have ascribed any unusual powers to these garments... would have hopelessly muddled the reader, and the poet had to invent an excuse for the hero's action." [53]

This "excuse" in *Guingamor* is as follows:

> Des que Guingamors l'ot veue,
> Conmeuz est de sa biauté;
> Le frain du cheval a tiré;
> Sor un grant arbre vit ses dras:
> Cele part vint, ne targe pas,
> El crues d'un chiesne les a mis:
> Quant il avra le sengler pris,
> Ariére vorra retorner
> Et a la pucele parler;
> Bien set qu'ele n'ira pas nue. (vv. 434-43)

Thus while in the *Dolopathos* the hero, as soon as he sees the fay, "ses chiens oublie et sa mainie," as does the hero in *Graelent*, in *Guingamor* the knight's first concern remains the boar. He wants to speak with the maiden, but only after the successful conclusion of his hunt, "quant il avra le sengler pris." In Schofield's opinion, this indicates only that "the situation is somewhat stupidly distorted," [54] and it is true that the fairy-mistress framework, according to which the boar should have served solely to bring the hero to the fay, cannot account for this preference. When the knight encounters the fay, the boar's role is supposedly terminated and the hunt itself, along with all else, should be forgotten. But Guingamor does not appear to know the rules of the game. We must conclude either that the author of the lay here produced a

---

[53] *Ibid.*, pp. 235-36.
[54] *Loc. cit.*

"stupidly distorted" version, or that the author had something else in mind. Is it possible that the boar is not to be considered simply as a "fairy messenger" sent by the fay to lead her chosen hero to her side? This is another question to be reconsidered.

Guingamor is now, like other heroes in similar works, in possession of the maiden's clothes. In the *Dolopathos*, where the swan-maiden nature of the heroine is evident, Schofield points out that " 'la demoiselle fu souprise' (v. 9252) and that was true." [55] *Graelent* too retains some traces of the swan-maiden capture, for the swan-maiden was always taken by surprise, and the fay says when the hero takes her clothes, "Graelent, vus m'avés surprise;" but this surprise can hardly be genuine, for she continues:

> 'Pur vus ving-jou à la fontaine,
> Pur vus souferai-jou grant paine;
> Bien savoie ceste aventure...' (vv. 315-17)

If these words of the fay are compared to those in episodes studied earlier in which the fay has long been interested in the hero and has guided his exploits, and combined with the fact that the white hart which mysteriously appears to the knight guides him directly to the fay, we see that in these particulars *Graelent* closely resembles the basic fairy-mistress tradition.

Schofield maintains that the fairy's relationship to the hero is the same in *Graelent* and in *Guingamor*. It is true that the first words of the maiden when she notices the knight taking her clothing are almost identical; in *Graelent*,

> Lor Dame l'a araisuné,
> Par mautalent l'a apelé:
> "Graelent, lai mes dras ester..." (vv. 229-31)

and in *Guingamor*:

> Le chevalier a apelé
> Et fiérement aresonné:
> "Guingamors, lessiez ma despoille..." (vv. 445-47)

---

[55] *Loc. cit.*

Schofield is also, as shown by the fact that both damsels at once call the knight by name, correct to note that "the maiden in *Guingamor* and in *Graelent* is in no way surprised by the knight's advent." [56] However, he attempts to extend the parallel: "She knows all about him —past and future— and is there on purpose to meet him." [57] That is true enough of *Graelent*, as the fay specifically states that it is true, but it is inaccurate with regard to *Guingamor*. Here the fay does know that the knight has been hunting without success, and that he must be weary, but she does *not* state that she has come in order to meet him. The omission is significant. We have noted that in some tales based on a fairy-mistress pattern, such as that of the *Biaus Desconeüs*, episodes which originally appear unconnected with the fairy influence later are found to have been arranged by the fay as part of her general supervision of the knight's activities. In such tales, however, the fairy eventually explains her role. In *Guingamor* one might expect the fairy at this point to reveal that it had been she who inspired the queen to suggest the boar-hunt, knowing that Guingamor would accept the challenge and be led to her. This would provide a standard fairy-link between the earlier introductory Potiphar's-wife episode and the encounter with the fay. However, no such link is furnished, and as before, we are left with two possible conclusions: that the author was too inept to unify his story, or that he had something else in mind.

The exact nature of the exchange between Guingamor and the fay also sets the poem apart. The knight is about to continue his pursuit of the boar, taking the damsel's clothing with the intention to return to her after the successful completion of his hunt, when she addresses him by name. She does of course urge him to leave her clothes, and her reasons are significant:

> "Guingamors, lessiez ma despoille.
> Ja Deu ne place ne ne voille
> Qu'entre chevaliers soit retret
> Que vos faciez si grant mesfet
> D'embler les dras d'une meschine
> En l'espoisse de la gaudine..." (vv. 447-52)

---

[56] *Ibid.*, p. 237.
[57] *Loc. cit.*

The emphasis here is, clearly, on the "mesfet" involved in Guingamor's action, rather than on its potential harm or inconvenience to the fay. How is this attempt at persuasion to be interpreted?

Schofield says of this fay that "once caught, it is she, of course, who commands," and adds that the hero "must humbly agree to whatever she decrees, for she has the greatest power."[58] This conclusion is apparently based on the assumption that what the author does not say, he at least intends, considering it obvious that the fairy is actually making the move which the tradition expects of her at this point, despite the phrasing of her request for the return of her clothes which tends to disguise the move to some extent. However, the fairy's words do not produce the impression of command. With courtly words she attempts to shame the knight for taking her clothes, making what is essentially an appeal to his better nature. She then invites him to stay with her, and Guingamor, easily persuaded by her words, at once returns her clothes. The reason for his compliance, however, cannot be that he is completely within her power, because, again forgetful of his role as the hero of a fairy-mistress tale, he declines her invitation:

> Guingamors est alé vers li,
> Ses dras li porta et tendi,
> De son offre la mercia,
> Et dit pas ne herbergera,
> Car il avoit son porc perdu
> Et le brachet qui l'a seu. (vv. 457-62)

Why is he such a recalcitrant hero? Damon has but one comment for this refusal: "What a stupid boy!"[59] In considering the lay primarily as a representative of the fairy-mistress type, Guingamor's attitude is difficult to explain.

The fay, however, apparently understands this determination of the knight to continue the hunt. She explains to him that it is "folie," since he will never succeed unaided:

---

[58] *Loc. cit.*

[59] S. Foster Damon, "Marie de France —Psychologist of Courtly Love," *PMLA*, XLIV (1929), 988.

> "Amis, tuit cil qui sont el mont
> Nu porroient hui mes trover,
> Tant ne s'en savroient pener,
> Se de moi n'aviez aie." (vv. 464-67)

It is apparent from these words that she does have power, but it is power over the boar, not necessarily over the knight; and even this does not entitle one to assume that she had sent the boar as a "messenger" to tempt Guingamor.

She then repeats her invitation, promising that she will return to him the brachet and give him the boar to take back to his country:

> "Venez o moi par tel covent,
> Et je vos promet loiaument
> Que le sengler pris vos rendrai
> Et le brachet vos baillerai
> A porter en vostre pais
> Jusqu'a tierz jor: je vos plevis." (vv. 469-74)

And this time he agrees, "Par tel covent con dit avez" (v. 477). He then asks her courteously for her love, and she, "sage et bien aprise," does not hesitate to grant it.

The knight and his new *amie* return to the "palès" which Guingamor had entered earlier, and find it now inhabited by many knights, "tex trois cenz ou plus" (v. 510), each with his *amie*. The reader is reminded of the castles in numerous romances where a number of knights are assembled, passing the time pleasantly while waiting to be liberated by some errant hero who can overcome the fairy spell which holds them captive. There is no hint here, however, of any captivity, and if the knights are in the *palès* due to a fairy "retention," we have no suggestion that it is against their will.

Although he agrees, on certain terms, to go with his new-found *amie*, Guingamor does not forget the object of his entry into the forest. He soon desires to take the brachet and the boar back to his uncle the king, and to relate his *aventure*. He seeks to leave only in order to complete this quest which he had undertaken, and "puis reperera a sa drue" (v. 538). Here again, the boar assumes an importance which is unexplained by its suggested role as a device to draw the hero to the fairy.[60]

The fay opposes the venture, explaining that although Guingamor is unaware of it, three hundred years have passed, and his uncle and all the court are dead. This supernatural passage of time in fairy-land is an element frequently found in tales involving voyages to the Otherworld, to be discussed in the following chapter. It is necessary to proceed with care in interpreting the fay's role in this. MacCulloch says of the fairies that their dwellings seem splendid and luxurious when seen by mortals, "but often all this proves to be mere glamour when the mortal comes to himself;" to this corresponds their power "of making time appear long or short to those mortals who are lured into their company."[61] In the typical fairy-mistress tale the hero is in fact lured into the company of the fairy, and is usually described as being "in her power" during his "retention" there. In such a case, every aspect of his stay in her company may properly be attributed to her influence. However, in *Guingamor* we have seen that such aspects of "luring," "power," and "retention" are minimized; in fact they do not appear at all, and if we are to assume them, we must base our assumptions upon the type of tale to which the lay belongs, and not upon the details of the lay itself. The passing of time described in the poem is subject to other explanations than that of the power of the fairy mistress exercised to detain her chosen knight.

Guingamor does not believe the fay when she tells him that three hundred years have passed since he left his uncle's court, but he promises to return at once if he finds it true. Acting the part of a good fairy mistress, his *amie* gives him a parting injunction, warning that he will suffer if he fails to obey it:

---

[60] Damon has suggested an explanation for the boar-hunt which makes of it the key element in the lay, based on the assumption that it is indeed the traditional device to draw the hero to the fay; however, as this explanation is not in terms of the fairy-mistress tradition itself, but rather of a symbolic interpretation of that entire tradition, Damon's proposals will be examined in the final chapter of this study.

[61] *Op. cit.*, p. 679.

> Ele li dist: "Je vos chasti,
> Quant la riviére avrez passée
> Por raler en vostre contrée,
> Que ne bevez ne ne mengiez
> Por nule fain que vos aiez,
> De si que serez reperiez:
> Tost en seriez engingniez." (vv. 564-70)

This commandment of the fay is not, like that in *Lanval*, *Graelent*, and other tales of the type, personal; it is not based on the fay's relationship to the knight. As has been noted, the injunction to secrecy which appears frequently in such tales was consistent with contemporary ideals of the conduct of amorous relationships. The commandment not to eat or drink while in the mortal world, on the other hand, is more similar to the injunctions in the older Celtic tales, and concerns the hero's well-being exclusively. In *Bran*, in *Connla* and in *Oisin*, merely touching the mortal earth after a lengthy stay in the Otherworld was enough to cause destruction, and it is about this that these heroes are warned. In the case of an injunction to secrecy, the fay herself has the power to inflict punishment for disobedience, by withholding her presence and her love; in *Guingamor* the lady is warning her *ami* about a fundamental rule which obtains between the world of mortals and the Otherworld, and the warning is given, not to demonstrate her power or to suit her whim, but to keep him from harm. She is warning him of punishment for breaking the commandment, not threatening him with it.

Guingamor, who cannot believe that her words are true, receives from her the boar's head and the brachet according to her promise, and journeys back to his own land. There he learns from a *charboniers* that three hundred years have indeed passed. He gives the *charboniers* the boar's head and instructs him to tell the story of the *aventure* to his countrymen, then turns, as he had promised, to make his way back to his *amie*. At this time, having passed the afternoon in the world of men, he feels a man's hunger, so severe that "il se cuida vif enragier" (v. 636). Seeing a wild-apple tree laden with fruit, he eats three apples, forgetful of the fay's warning. The consequences which she had predicted follow instantly:

> Si tost comme il en ot gouté,
> Tost fu desfez et envielliz,
> Et de son cors si afoibliz
> Que du cheval l'estut cheoir;
> Ne pot ne pié ne main avoir. (vv. 644-48)

This aging after eating the wild apples has been given an explanation in terms of folklore. Schofield quotes Child, that "eating and drinking, personal contact, exchange of speech, receiving of gifts, in any abode of unearthly beings, including the dead, will reduce a man to their fellowship and condition..."[62] The theme has been expressed in similar terms by E. Philipot: "Quiconque prend ou accepte un fruit dans un lieu surnaturel (île enchantée, demeure des morts, paradis, etc...) entre, d'une façon définitive ou sous réserves, dans les conditions d'existence assignées aux habitants de ce lieu; il reste lié à la terre dont il a pris le fruit." Philipot assembles more examples of this theme: the serpent of Genesis telling Eve that by eating the apple she might become like God himself, the myth of Persephone who must remain in the kingdom of Hades after eating the fruit of the realm of the dead, etc.[63]

There are magic orchards in *Erec*, the *Biaus Desconeüs*, the *Livre d'Artus* and other romances which are survivals of this theme. That in the *Livre d'Artus* Philipot considers to be of particular relevance to Guingamor. It is the work of an enchantress, the Queen of Danemark. A "molt biau jardin ou il avoit arbres de toutes manieres de fruiz," it has in its center an apple tree heavy with red apples. The knight Agravain accepts to eat of the apple tree, and at once "se sent pris d'une envie irrésistible de demeurer là pour toujours;" he then recognizes the nine companions of the Round Table, "prisonniers comme lui, et comme lui heureux de leur prison." Later the captive knights are freed by others who refuse to eat the apple. As Philipot notes, "le seul fait de goûter à la pomme du verger paradisiaque met les survenants dans la condition des premiers arrivés, autrement dit à la merci des auteurs de l'enchantement. Ils deviennent prison-

---

[62] "Guingamor," p. 224.
[63] "Un Episode d'Erec et Enide," *Romania*, XXV (1896), 272.

niers, dans le sens le plus complet du mot, non seulement prisonniers de fait, mais encore de pensées et de désir: l'enchantement a saisi leur être tout entier..."[64]

This is of importance in relation to *Guingamor*, says Philipot, because it suggests answers to two puzzling questions which had been raised by Gaston Paris at the time of his publication of the lay. In the first place, there is the obvious fact, pointed out by Paris, that *Guingamor* presents the *opposite* of this widespread theme —as Schofield has it, "but another, though inverted, instance of a well-known superstition."[65] The hero is not brought under the fairy spell by eating magic fruit, but rather returns abruptly to his mortal state by eating fruit in the land of mortals. Philipot offers as an explanation that "la légende complète comprenait l'autre partie et que le héros goûtait au fruit des fées avant de devenir leur hôte." He goes further; in answer to the second question raised by Paris, concerning the ten knights who had undertaken the pursuit of the boar before Guingamor and whom the hero found in the enchanted palace, he suggests "que ce sont des prisonniers féeriques, comme les *dix* prisonniers de la reine de Danemark (neuf, plus Agravain), qui, eux aussi, appartenaient à la cour d'Artus. Ils mènent d'ailleurs joyeuse vie et semblent se complaire dans une captivité égayée par des jeux, des chants, la musique des harpes et des violes."[66]

Again we find, in the study of a work of a particular type, the assumption that if the author of the work did not include a detail which is frequently found in stories of that type, he must at least have intended it, omitting it only through oversight or through ineptitude in handling his material. The fact that the poem in question does in fact present an episode which seems to be the exact *opposite* of that expected leaves little doubt in the scholar's mind that he is correct. On this basis correspondences are suggested —based on the *assumed*, not the *existing*, poem— which force upon the latter interpretations which within

---

[64] *Ibid.*, pp. 272-74.
[65] "Guingamor," p. 224. Schofield's study is acute in noting elements which seem to depart from the tradition, but the analysis of these elements is always in terms of the tradition itself.
[66] *Op. cit.*, p. 274.

its own context are highly questionnable. In the present case the suggested connection of *Guingamor* with the *Livre d'Artus*, in which the knights who are joyous residents of the "molt biau jardin" are in fact prisoners of an enchantress, forces upon *Guingamor* the interpretation that the ten knights from Arthur's court, and the hero himself, are all likewise prisoners, kept in blissful ignorance of their captivity by means of a magic spell. But this, if one may answer an argument from type with another argument from type, is to confuse two types of fairy-mortal relationships. The Queen of Danemark in the *Livre d'Artus* is a wicked enchantress who established her magic garden "par nicromance," having vowed to dispose of all the knights of the Kingdom of Logres,[67] whereas the fay in *Guingamor* is "sage et bien aprise," and shows only courtesy toward the hero, with no indication of malevolence. Her very command as he takes his leave is a warning to keep him from a great danger of which she alone is aware.

Schofield, whose study of *Guingamor* is generally full of insight, also fails to come to terms with this puzzling apple incident. As noted above, he calls it "but another, though inverted, instance of a well-known superstition," not inquiring whether the inversion itself may not be precisely the significant element. He later advances an alternative to Philipot's supposition that the complete legend comprised both parts. It is equally likely, he says, that "the present position of this feature in our account is due to an accidental shifting of it from its more usual place at the beginning of the supernatural life. Possibly it was intentionally put where it is by the poet, who may have thought this a better way of explaining the transformation of Guingamor than the older one of mere contact with the earth, as in *Bran, Connla,* and *Oisin.*"[68]

The poem's conclusion conforms to the pattern of the typical fairy-mistress lay. The hero falls from his horse after his transgression, hardly able to speak, and the *charboniers* watches him in alarm:

---

[67] See *Ibid.*, p. 272.
[68] "Guingamor," p. 225. This is the most pertinent point in Schofield's mention of this episode, but here again he fails to ask *why* the poet might have thought this a better explanation.

> Bien voit con li est avenu;
> Ne cuidoit mie au sien espoir
> Qu'il peust vivre jusqu'au soir... (vv. 652-54)

Two damsels, probably the traditional attendants of the fay, "de riche ator et bien vestues" (v. 657), approach. They dismount beside Guingamor and reproach him for his failure to keep the fay's commandment. Then they lead him away:

> Belement et souef l'ont pris,
> Si l'ont sor un cheval asis,
> A la riviére le menérent,
> En un bastel outre passérent
> Son brachet en son chaceor. (vv. 663-67)

All of this conforms to the pattern of the hero's last-moment rescue from the consequences of breaking the commandment of his *amie*. However, in comparing it with the corresponding conclusions to *Lanval* and *Graelent*, two significant differences appear. In the first place, there is no indication here, as in the other two lays, of the fay's anger. In *Lanval* and *Graelent* her reaction to being disobeyed takes the form of temporary desertion of her knight, to the extent that in both cases he is seriously endangered by her refusal to appear. It is true that in *Guingamor* the two damsels do not fail to mention the knight's transgression:

> Molt blamérent le chevalier
> Et commencent a reprouchier
> Le commandement trespassé,
> Que mauvesement l'a gardé... (vv. 659-62)

Their reproach does not seem, however, to be made in anger, and is clearly appropriate in the light of the consequences to the knight himself of his disobedience. Their immediate appearance when the knight's life is endangered as a result of his disobedience is a further indication that their reproach does not indicate the fairy's wrath; the mistresses of Lanval and Graelent made no haste to come to the rescue of the disobedient *ami*.

A second point of divergence is the actual fate of the hero as related in the conclusion. In *Graelent* the fay finally takes pity on her knight, and carries him off with her to her own land. In *Lanval* the hero's happy destination is quite specific: leaping onto the palfrey behind his *amie*,

> Od li s'en vait en Avalun,
> Ceo nus recuntent li Bretun,
> En un isle que mut est beaus;
> La fu ravi li dameiseaus. (vv. 641-44)

Guingamor's fate, in contrast, is left somewhat in doubt. In the other two lays the restoration of the fay's favor, her forgiveness of the knight's disobedience, was the necessary factor in ensuring his future happiness. In *Guingamor*, however, it is never implied that the hero fell from the favor of his *amie*; he has transgressed against something more fundamental than her personal wishes. We are left uncertain, therefore, as to whether the remedy is in her power. Brugger, considering the line by Wauchier referring to Guingamor's fate "Bien avés oï qu'il devient," feels no doubt as to the lay's conclusion: "nach dem Lai musste man annehmen dass er vom Tode gerettet wurde." [69] But all we are told specifically is that the hero is carried away, on the verge of death; he is presumably to rejoin the fay, and this second entry into the fairy Otherworld differs radically from the joyous return there of Graelent and of Lanval.

The rest of the lay is traditional, according to formula. The *aventure* becomes known, when the *charboniers* takes the head of the boar to the king and tells its story throughout the land as Guingamor had instructed him: "Par serement l'aferme et jure." The king exhibits the boar's head at many a gathering; and then

> Por l'aventure recorder
> En fist li rois un lai trover:
> De Guingamor retint le non;
> Einsi l'apelent li Breton. (vv. 675-78)

The study of *Guingamor* as a fairy-mistress lay reveals it to be in some ways typical. It also reveals that by considering it

---

[69] E. Brugger, "Eigennamen in den Lais der Marie de France," *ZFSL*, XLIX (1927), 214, n. 26.

exclusively as such, many questions remain unanswered. Scholars have generally considered the fairy-mistress aspect the most important, and therefore the determining, element in *Guingamor*, and have thus concluded that these unanswered questions result from ineptitude on the part of the poet. In the final chapter of this study the questions will be raised again, to see whether an as yet unattempted defense for the poet may not be made.

CHAPTER II

GUINGAMOR: AN OTHERWORLD-VOYAGE LAY

H. Zimmer in an early contribution to the study of Arthurian names noted four mentions of the name Guingamor or a variant, in the *Erec*, the *Bel Inconnu*, Marie's *Guigemar*, and the *Perceval*, and pointed out their basic similarity: "In allen vier Fällen treffen wir dieselben beiden Hauptpersonen des Abenteurs, den Helden *Guingamor* (*Guigemar*, *Guingamuer*) und seine *amie* die *fee*, und dasselbe Sagenmotiv, Aufenthalt eines Sterblichen bei einer Fee in einem Wunderland (Wunderinsel)."[1] Other scholars too have recognized that the lay *Guingamor* is basically a combination of the themes of the Journey to the Otherworld and the Fairy Mistress.[2] Having considered *Guingamor* in the preceding chapter as a member of the fairy-mistress classification, we may now consider the Otherworld motif and attempt to determine its relative importance and its function in the poem.

The concept of the Otherworld is a broad one, and for the purposes of this study it is important to determine what sort of Otherworld idea is presented in *Guingamor*. Three varieties of Otherworld frequently appear as elements in the lay and romance material: the Celtic Otherworld, the Arthurian Otherworld, and these as colored by Christian Otherworld conceptions. These

---

[1] "Beiträge zur Namenforschung in den altfranzösische Arthurepen," *ZFSL*, XIII, i (1891), 8.
[2] See, for example, Cross on *Lanval* and *Graelent*. For a further discussion of this "offended *Fée*" and her relation to these motifs, see this author's article "The Celtic 'Fée' in *Launfal*," *Kittredge Anniversary Papers* (Boston, 1923), 377-87.

types frequently are not clearly distinguishable in the medieval romances. On the contrary, the general concept of the Otherworld having great appeal as a theme, medieval authors tended to borrow features from one concept or another as the development of their particular tale seemed to require.

The tales which express each of these three Otherworld conceptions are usually accounts of a voyage to the Otherworld by some hero or group of heroes, with the result that the actual description or discussion of the Otherworld itself is frequently subordinated to concerns which we may term those of "plot"— why a certain mortal is privileged to visit the Otherworld, how he reaches it, how he is treated there, how (if at all) he returns to the mortal world, possibly also the changes brought about in him as a result of his voyage. Both elements, description and function in plot, are relevant to the study of *Guingamor*, and they may best be considered separately.

A purely Celtic conception of the Otherworld is difficult to discover and to characterize with any precision, in part because the earliest extant texts are probably composite, showing an admixture of Christian elements. Alfred Nutt notes, in elaborating his approach to the Irish Otherworld as expressed in literature, that the isolating of elements purely Celtic in nature is a complex task. First the relation of "the remains of our text to such other remains of Irish literature as contain similar scenes and ideas must be determined, and the paradise ideal of the ancient Irish must be reconstructed. This ideal must be set by the side of beliefs and poetic imagining, found firstly in Graeco-Roman literature, secondly in that of other Aryan races."[3] Such an undertaking far surpasses the scope of the present study, but it is possible, by noting the references to the Otherworld in several early texts, to arrive at a few generally accepted characteristics.

Four early texts, the stories of the experiences of the Irish heroes Bran, Connla, Oisin, and Cuchulinn, contain rather consistent presentations of the Otherworld. Professor Nutt was of the opinion that these tales represented the main road of Gaelic literature, while the better-known *imrama* were but a bypath; in

---

[3] *Op. cit.*, p. 134.

his opinion, the *imrama* are later, and show "the indefiniteness of an artificial literary *genre*, which has discarded the mould into which the imagination of the race had previously been cast, with a view to acquiring greater freedom and increased capacities;" with the earlier hero stories, on the other hand, "we remain in a world of mythic fantasy in which the *imrama* have little part." [4]

The *Voyage of Bran*, considered by Kuno Meyer to be one of the oldest remains of Irish story-telling, [5] contains in its verse portions significant descriptions of the Otherworld visited by the hero. A mysterious woman comes to seek Bran in his house and sings to him of the delights of the Otheworld. These delights are basically of two kinds: the physical beauty of the place, with an abundance of all good things, and the joyous way of life enjoyed by those who dwell there. The physical attributes are introduced in the form of a mysterious branch of an apple tree which the woman gives to Bran. The Otherworld itself is described as an island, a lovely land "throughout the world's age" (6), [6] bright with color:

> Colors glisten with pure glory
> A fair stream of silver, cloths of gold,
> Afford a welcome with all abundance. (40)

The way of life of the inhabitants, too, is presented in the verses. They are often engaged in contests, and pass their time "listening to sweet music, Drinking the best of wine." (13)

> A beautiful game, most delightful,
> They play (sitting) at the luxurious wine,
> Men and gentle women under a bush,
> Without sin, without crime. (41)

---

[4] *Ibid.*, p. 173.

[5] The verse portion is probably older than the prose; Meyer regards its language as "coeval with the earliest recorded glosses, in other words, to belong, possibly, to the eighth or even to the seventh century" (*Bran*, p. 135).

[6] The numbers included in parentheses are quatrain numbers in the Meyer translation of the *Voyage of Bran*.

"Sin" and "crime" are completely absent from life in the Otherworld, the moral qualities of which are emphasized equally with the physical delights.

> We are from the beginning of creation
> Without old age, without consummation of earth,
> Hence we expect not that there should be frailty,
> The sin has not come to us. (44)

All is harmony; "calves and colored lambs" are together "with friendliness, without mutual slaughter." (38)

> Unknown is wailing or treachery
> In the familiar cultivated land,
> There is nothing rough or harsh,
> But sweet music striking on the ear. (9)

Its happy inhabitants are, furthermore, deathless:

> Without grief, without sorrow, without death,
> Without any sickness, without debility,
> That is the sign of Emain—
> Uncommon is an equal marvel. (10)

Thus the major characteristic of the Otherworld as presented in this early text is its combination of sensuous and moral qualities: its beauty and abundance, and the harmony of the immortal life of its residents, who "enjoy in full measure a simple round of sensuous delights." [7]

Connla's invitation to the Otherworld is presented by a fairy damsel whom we have met in the previous chapter. She invites him to the Plain of Delight, where, she says, he will enjoy eternal youth. She urges him to leave his mortal companions because "Tis no lofty seat on which Connla sits among short-lived mortals awaiting fearful death. The ever-living living ones invite thee." [8] She then tells him "of another land, in which there is no race save only women and maidens." [9] The ultimate destination of Bran

---

[7] Nutt, p. 143.
[8] *Ibid.*, p. 145.
[9] *Ibid.*, p. 146.

was called the Isle of Fair Women, and as Nutt points out, "substantially the presentment of the Happy Otherworld is the same in both tales." [10]

A third story describing the Otherworld is that of Oisin, [11] also studied in the previous chapter for its presentation of a fairy mistress. The damsel who persuades Oisin to depart with her describes the Otherworld to which she wishes to take him:

> Abundant there are honey and wine,
> And aught else the eye has beheld.
> Fleeting time shall not bend thee,
> Death nor decay shalt thou see. [12]

Again, physical delight, physical abundance; again, immortality.

Yet another Irish hero, Cuchulinn, is summoned to the Otherworld. The country to which he is invited is the Plain of Delight, located on an island. Life there is joyful, reports the man whom the hero sends before him:

> There is a vat there of merry mead,
> A-distributing unto the household,
> Still it remains, constant the custom,
> So that it is ever full, even and always.

So delightful is it, in fact, that the messenger declares:

> If all Erin were mine
> And the kingship of yellow Bregia,
> I would give it all, no trifling deed,
> To dwell for aye in the place I reached. [13]

Nutt says of the *imrama* literature that "of all classes of ancient Irish mythic fiction this is the most famous and the one which has most directly affected the remainder of West European liter-

---

[10] *Ibid.*, p. 149.
[11] *Ibid.*, p. 151. In Nutt's opinion it should be considered with the stories of Bran and Connla because, although preserved only in an eighteenth-century form, it represents "early component parts of the Fenian cycle."
[12] *Ibid.*, p. 150.
[13] *Ibid.*, p. 135.

ature." [14] The *imrama* is composite; its most famous example, the *Voyage of Saint Brandan*, "is the latest and a definitely Christian example of a genre of story-telling which had already flourished for centuries in Ireland, when it seemed good to an unknown writer to dress the old half-Pagan marvels in orthodox monkish garb, and thus start them afresh on their triumphal march through the literature of the world." [15] The *Voyage of Maelduin* is probably the oldest of the existing *imrama* tales, "the model upon which and the quarry out of which the later *imrama*, and notably Saint Brandan's Voyage, were built." [16] When Maelduin and his companions in their wandering reach the island which provides a partial parallel to the Otherworld islands visited by other heroes, they are offered baths, food and drink, and the company of a fair damsel for each. There are in the *Voyage of Maelduin* also two other islands of fair damsels which the hero visits, both of which disappear mysteriously. All are much the same as the Otherworld visited by Bran: "The mortal visitor is welcomed to the same perpetual round of simple sensuous delights; he shall not age, he shall not decay, he shall have the savour of whatever food pleases him, he shall enjoy love, in undiminished vigour, 'without labours'; the supernatural nature of the land is apparent..." [17]

A different body of Irish myth, centering about the fairy-folk of Tuatha De Danaan (the folk of the Goddess Dana), presents a type of Otherworld life quite different from the peaceful and harmonious one already encountered, and the turbulent existence attributed to the fairy-folk seems to have had little influence in literary tradition, although it survives in popular superstition. This body of myth is of interest, however, for two reasons. First, it presents substantially the same picture of the enjoyment of sensuous delight in the Otherworld as that found in all the accounts examined previously. In addition, the position of the Otherworld is important. It is not located on an island, but is rather to be found in the fairy-mound, in the hollow hill. The land of the fairy-folk,

---

[14] *Ibid.*, p. 161.
[15] *Loc. cit.*
[16] *Ibid.*, p. 162.
[17] *Ibid.*, p. 166.

then, "though in Ireland is not in mortal Ireland;"[18] thus we have in the legends of the Tuatha De Danaan a conception of the Otherworld as coexisting with the mortal world, an Otherworld land upon which one may come unexpectedly, a land which may not be recognized as the Otherworld until one is within —a land which may be visited by chance, without having to be sought.

The consideration of how one may arrive at the Celtic Otherworld introduces the "plot" aspect of the Otherworld accounts— how a hero is permitted to visit the Otherworld, and what happens to him during and as a result of his stay there. Bran, Connla, Oisin, Cuchulinn —all were invited to visit the Otherworld by a damsel who came to seek the hero in the world of mortals. Maelduin happens upon what Nutt terms the "island of the amorous queen" in the course of his lengthy *imrama*, and receives a welcome there comparable to that enjoyed by the earlier heroes. In all of these accounts the supernatural maiden is most anxious to give the hero her love and to retain him. However, the return to the mortal world of all the heroes except Connla is described, and the circumstances and results of this return are important. Bran is persuaded to go by one of his kinsmen seized with homesickness; this kinsman leaps from the coracle as the wanderers near Ireland, and is turned to ashes, causing Bran to sing that "for Collbran's son great was the folly To lift his hand against age." (65) Oisin himself longs to see his mortal land, and when he touches the earth there, becomes an old man. On the other hand, Cuchulinn when he returns to his own land at the insistence of his wife Emer apparently suffers no ill effects; and although the fairy in Maelduin's voyage is so determined to retain him that his departure is an "escape,"[19] he suffers no apparent harm and continues his episodic voyage. Nutt considers that the difficulty of return from the Otherworld is a definite part of the early Celtic conception, absent from the Cuchulinn account only because "the main outlines of the Cuchulinn saga were probably fixed before the episode was worked into it."[20] The absence of this important Otherworld characteristic in the *imrama* may be similarly explained,

---

[18] *Ibid.*, p. 175.
[19] For the account of this departure, see *ibid.*, p. 165.
[20] *Ibid.*, p. 160.

if Nutt is correct in assuming that the *imrama* literature represents the Otherworld conception in a much later stage of development than that in *Bran* or *Connla*.

Combining the two aspects of the Otherworld and Voyage, then, the early Irish tales present these essential elements: the Otherworld is a place where one may enjoy both "simple sensuous pleasures" and deathlessness; it is a place difficult of access, which only specially chosen or privileged mortals may visit; and once one has entered and enjoyed the life there, return to the mortal world is perilous, if not impossible.

The Otherworld concept as represented in Welsh tradition is very similar in its essential characteristics to that found in the Irish tales, although "il est incontestable que ce sont les Irlandais qui ont le mieux conservé la tradition celtique primitive."[21] For example, *Branwen Daughter of Llyr* of the *Mabinogi* presents as one of its episodes a sojourn on an island called Gwales which strongly resembles the Otherworld islands visited by Irish heroes. A group of men in *Branwen* had been commanded by their leader before his death to go to Gwales and to refrain from opening one of the three doors of the great hall which they would find. On their arrival, "ils y trouvèrent un endroit agréable, royal, audessus des flots, et une grande salle... Ils y passèrent la nuit au milieu de l'abondance et de la gaieté. Quoi qu'ils eussent vu de souffrance, quoi qu'ils en eussent éprouvé eux-mêmes, ils ne se rappelèrent rien, non plus qu'aucun chagrin au monde. Ils y passèrent quatre-vingts années de telle sorte qu'ils ne se rappelaient pas avoir eu un meilleur temps ni plus agréable dans toute leur vie. Ils n'étaient pas plus fatigués; aucun d'eux ne s'apercevait que l'autre fut plus vieux de tout ce temps qu'au moment où ils y étaient venus." After the eighty years, however, one of them is determined to open the forbidden door "pour savoir si ce qu'on dit est vrai." He does so, and at once "toutes les pertes qu'ils avaient faites, la mort de leurs parents et de leurs compagnons, tout le mal qui leur était arrivé leur revint en mémoire aussi clairement que si tout fût survenu à ce moment même... A partir de ce moment, ils n'eurent pas de repos..."[22]

---

[21] J. Loth, ed., *Les Mabinogion* (Paris, 1931), I, 45.
[22] *Ibid.*, pp. 148-49.

In a study of *Bran the Blessed*, Helaine Newstead has pointed out the similarities between *Branwen* and two poems about Caer Siddi ("fairy fortress") found in the *Book of Taliesin*. In the first of these poems the bard Taliesin says he dwells there:

> Perfect is my seat in Caer Siddi.
> Nor plague nor age harms him who dwells therein...
> Around its corners ocean's currents flow,
> And above it is the fertile fountain,
> And sweeter than white wine is the drink therein.

Newstead is of the opinion that there are enough significant correspondences between Gwales and the poet's Caer Siddi to suggest their probable identification in Welsh tradition. Both are located in the sea; the same heroes are said to participate in both episodes; aging is absent from both; both refer to marvellous food.[23]

A second Taliesin poem also mentioning Caer Siddi is a "somewhat obscure account of an expedition to the Otherworld" called the *Preiddeu Annwn*, and its description also is of a Happy Otherworld or Elysium:

> Complete was the captivity of Gwair in Caer Siddi...
> In the four-cornered fortress, in quick-door island...
> The sparkling wine their drink before their retinue...[24]

Of greater interest in this second poem referring to Caer Siddi is a mention of Arthur: "Before the fortress of glass they had not seen Arthur's valor...", indicating the connection between the Celtic Otherworld and Arthurian tradition. From this discussion of Caer Siddi to the Arthurian Otherworld, the distance is not great.

The conception of the Otherworld found in the *matière de Bretagne* is strongly derivative, and, like so many other elements of Arthurian romance, its derivation has been the subject of dispute. There are in fact two general Otherworld conceptions to be found in the romance tradition. The first is what we may

---

[23] *Bran the Blessed in Arthurian Romance* (New York, 1939), 24-5.
[24] *Loc. cit.*

term *faërie*—any place of enchantment, the "fairy" world as distinguished from the mortal world. The second, and the object of much scholarly investigation, is Avalon, which is as Lucy Paton notes "the otherworld *par excellence* in the 'matter of Britain'." [25] Elements of these two conceptions, while often found in conjunction, may to some extent be isolated.

Faërie has many forms; it may be termed *Ile Celée, Terre Lointaine, Forêt sans Retor, Val sans Retor, Ile d'Or, Chastel as Pucièles*—none of these used in a generic sense. Paton, pointing out that "in fairyland, the pleasures are sensuous in their quality: —splendid dwellings, gay colors, feasts where the viands gratify each hero's particular taste, the best of wine, sweet music, a marvellously beautiful woman," [26] appears to identify Faërie with the Celtic Otherworld, on the basis of the resemblances between it and such islands as the Plain of Delight in these respects. We have seen, however, that in addition to sensuous qualities, the Celtic Otherworld conception in so far as we have succeeded in isolating it emphasized also a different set of qualities —harmony, freedom from sin, deathlessness— which may or may not accompany the delights of Faërie in any given instance.

In fact Faërie seems to have no specific characteristics other than the marvellous; the *Val sans Retor* is not the *Terre Lointaine*, nor is it the *Chastel as Pucièles*; its characteristics depend on the reason for its existence. The *Val sans Retor*, for example, is according to the *Livre d'Artus*, P. established by Morgain as a result of her resentment against the queen and her love for the hero Guiomar. Paton notes that with the *Val sans Retor* "we are dealing distinctly with an other-world adventure. Merely the name of the valley is enough to indicate this, and its important features may all be paralleled from other-world scenes." [27] Philipot has noted that it belongs to the same type of region as the enchanted castle of mist imprisoning the Noir Chevalier in the *Perceval* continuation; the enchanted garden of the Queen of Danemark in the *Livre d'Artus*, P.; the garden of the *Joie de la Cour* in *Erec*; and the air-bounded prison of Merlin in the *Merlin*

---

[25] *Op. cit.*, p. 40.
[26] *Loc. cit.*
[27] *Ibid.*, p. 83.

romances.[28] In another article he has studied the *Mabon l'enchanteur* episode of the *Biaus Desconeüs* in its similarities to the *Joie de la Cour*,[29] to which Paton adds another example: Urbain's imprisonment in the invisible castle in the *Didot-Perceval*.[30]

The point of great importance, however, is that the Celtic Otherworld conception as we are able to reconstruct it was not simply that of a non-mortal or magical place; it was a unified conception in which certain details were found in conjunction. Any particular manifestation of Faërie, on the other hand, is dependent on the whims of the fay who is responsible for it, and the only generality of which we may be certain is that it is always in some way "other" than the world of mortal men. It is an interesting endeavour to attempt to trace its varying details, but a consistent conception is not to be found.

Avalon, the second type of Otherworld of the Arthurian material, sometimes appears as an equivalent of Faërie. When Marie describes the hero Lanval as carried off to Avalon, it is the fairy Otherworld that she intends to evoke, "un isle qui mult est beals." However, Paton notes that "the number of passages is comparatively small that do not mention it particularly as the place where Arthur sought healing for his wound received at Camlan,"[31] and it is for its relation to Arthur that Avalon is best known.

The Isle of Avalon first appears in the *Historia regum Britanniae* of Geoffrey of Monmouth, where it is briefly mentioned twice. William of Malmesbury explains that the name derives from either the association with *poma*, or the association with a certain Avalloc who inhabited the island with his daughters, and modern scholars have in their discussion of the island's origins generally taken sides in support of one of these two interpretations.[32] In the *Vita Merlini* the island refuge of Arthur is again

---

[28] In *Romania*, XXVII (1898), 259.
[29] "Erec et Enide;" the article is a study of this episode and of parallels.
[30] *Op. cit.*, p. 209.
[31] *Ibid.*, p. 40, n. 2.
[32] For discussion of the derivation of the name, see E. Faral, *La Légende Arthurienne, Etudes et Documents* (Paris, 1929), I; F. Lot, "Etudes sur la provenance du cycle arthurien," *Romania*, XXIV (1895) and "Nouvelles Etudes sur la provenance du cycle arthurien," *Romania*, XXVII (1898); J. Rhys, *Studies*, pp. 337-338; E. Freymond, "Beitrage zur Kenntnis

mentioned, this time at greater length; it is not known as Avallo, however, but rather as the *Insula Pomorum*:

> Insula Pomorum, quae Fortunata vocatur,
> Ex re nomen habet, quia per se singula profert
> Non opus est illi sulcantibus arva colonis;
> Omnis abest cultus, nisi quem natura ministrat...
> Illuc post bellum Camblani, vulnere laesum,
> Ducimus Arcturum, nos conducente Barintho,
> Aequora cui fuerant et caeli sidera nota.

Faral points out that most of the elements in this description may be found in "des notices consacrées par des auteurs anciens à certains îles célèbres," and that Barinthus is taken from the Latin text of the *Navigatio sancti Brendani* in which the navigator reveals to the saint the Isle of Delights and "l'Ile de la Répromission des saints, qu'il avait lui-même visitées." [33]

Louis Cons attempts to determine the nature of Geoffrey's island according to the author's own description. In the *Historia* he finds it to be "une île magique où on ressuscite des gens mortellement blessés (*letaliter vulneratus*)," while the details of the description in the *Vita Merlini* vv. 908-942 "ne sont que broderie sur le thème de l'Historia." [34] Cons notes the medieval tradition of a "happy island," the "Ile Heureuse" of Isidore replaced by the Celtic image of an "Ile des Pommes," appearing frequently in folklore; there is a similar Biblical and clerical tradition, found for example in the glosses of St. Benedict where the apple represents the Earthly Paradise. [35] Unlike fairyland, the island provides delights of the sort scattered by nature, and, admits Paton, "far more than it resembles fairyland this island resembles the Fortunate Isles. In fact the description of the Fortunate Isles given by Rabanus Maurus so closely parallels that of the *Vita*

---

der altfranzösische Artusromane in Prosa," *ZFSL*, XVII (1895), p. 17, n. 4; Zimmer, "Beitrage zur Namenforschung"; F. M. Warren, "Avalon," *MLN*, XIV (1899).

[33] *Op. cit.*, p. 249. See also C. H. Slover, "Avalon," *MP*, XXVIII (1931), 395-99. Slover concludes from the introduction of Barinthus as a guide that we may assume that Geoffrey conceived of Avalon as an island paradise.

[34] "Avallo," *MP*, XXVIII (1931), 388.

[35] *Ibid.*, p. 394.

Merlini that the first eight verses of our passage read almost like a versification of the account of Rabanus." [36]

Wace added to the mention of Arthur's departure from the mortal world into Avalon the notion of the "Breton hope," the eventual return of Arthur. In his conservative fashion, Wace does not elaborate, nor does he repeat Geoffrey's reference to Morgain; not before Layamon's version of the *Brut* do we find an elaboration of the story. In his account Paton considers one element to be "somewhat foreign" with reference to the tradition. The fay's summons of the hero to fairyland, which he relates, is a theme which appears early in the fairy-mistress material; but the hero of Layamon's version is wounded, whereas the fay is usually attracted only to the strongest and most able knight. She is often represented as a healer, and Morgain is specified as the fay who attempts to cure the wounds of Arthur; but "when she comes upon the scene as a healer she is usually engaged in a beneficent rather than an amatory errand... The only source in which the love-motive is defined is the late *Gesta Regum Britanniae*, where the result of the king's healing is nothing more or less than a fairy imprisonment exercised by the queen of the other-world island, whither he had gone: 'sanati membra reservat ipsa sibi; vivuntque simul si credere fas est'." [37]

There is in fact another Latin account, chronologically near that of Layamon, which does not represent Morgain as either the sister of Arthur or a dignified *nobile matrona quadam*. It is that of Gervasius of Tilbury in the *Otia Imperialia*:

> Arcturus vulneratur, omnibus hostibus ab ipso peremptis. Unde secundum vulgarem Brittonum traditionem in insulam Davalim ipsum dicunt translatum ut vulnera quotannis recrudescentia subinterpolata sanatione curarentur a Morganda fatata: quem fabulose Britones post data tempora credunt rediturum in regnum. [38]

---

[36] *Op. cit.*, p. 41.

[37] *Ibid.*, pp. 28-29. The prototype of the two quite different relationships, of Arthur-Morgain and of Layamon's Arthur-Argante, is to be found, Paton suggests, in the Cuchulinn-Fand story.

[38] Ed. Leibnitz, I, 937; quoted in Paton, p. 35.

Here the damsel who is to cure the wounds of Arthur is simply "Morganda fatata," and the relationship is not specified.

The examples from Layamon and Gervasius indicate that the fairy-mistress element may be present in a fairy-plus-hero story in which the main emphasis of the relationship between fairy and hero is of some other type. The writer of romance was not limited to the fairy-loves-hero *or* fairy-heals-hero alternatives.

The conceptions of both types of Otherworld relevant to the Arthurian tradition, Faërie and Avalon, were affected by contact with Christianity. In considerations of this influence, the tendency to transform fairies into devils is frequently stressed. G. L. Kittredge says that "philosophy and Christianity account for the phenomena of fairy stories as diabolical illusions." [39] A. C. L. Brown ascribes to this tendency some of the "contemptuous epithets" directed at the *Britonum fabulae*, epithets such as those of Giraldus Cambrensis; the spirits which Giraldus mentions in an anecdote as settling upon Geoffrey's book are thus fairies, who were "drawn to the book not only because it was false, but because it was false in a special way, namely, its sources were unorthodox: *De Prestigiis Daemonum*." [40] E. Philipot offers as explanation for the fact that, especially in the prose romances, the fays are "en général peu sympathiques" that "lorsque le souvenir des belles légendes des paradis sensuels se fut effacé peu à peu, et qu'on s'avisa de juger les fées au nom de la morale, on fut sévère pour elles." [41]

Brown's description of the development of Arthurian romance gives a very large place to the evolution of fairy stories as a source of constantly fascinating material. "To dignify them for the cultivated reader," Brown suggests, "fairy stories must be made a vehicle for the social ideals of the age. Chrétien more than any other known author accomplished this feat... Finally, it was probably inevitable that the fairy stories should be connected with the story of Christ. These changes are all brought about

---

[39] *A Study of Gawain and the Green Knight* (Cambridge, Mass., 1920), 239.

[40] "A Note on the *Nugae* of G. H. Gerould's 'King Arthur and Politics'," *Speculum*, II (1927), 451.

[41] *Op. cit.*, pp. 281-82.

by a desire to dignify fairy stories which are too charming to be forgotten, and to make them appeal to the intellect and moral sense, as well as to the fancy, of people of the time." [42]

The contradiction between the two common treatments of fairy material, the "regular medieval transformation of fairies to devils" and the inevitability that "fairy stories should be connected with the story of Christ," is in fact only apparent. If fairy stories were of great interest, and we have the evidence of medieval literature that they were, an age preoccupied with Christianity and accustomed to seeking interpretations relevant to Christianity in works both religious and secular was certain to seek to relate the body of fairy mythology to Christian tradition. This effort was naturally not systematic, and might take either —or both— of two equally plausible directions. On the one hand, the fairy supernatural, not explicable in terms of the Christian supernatural, might be equated with the work of the devil. In the Christian view, whatever is not of God is of the devil, and unless the fairies could somehow be made to appear Christian their position in the hierarchy of creation was obvious. As C. Grant Loomis pointed out in his discussion of white magic, "the folklore of the operations of magic within Christianity has been studied more widely from the aspect of *maleficium*, than from the view of *beneficium*." [43]

On the other hand, the Church has tended throughout its history to assimilate elements which were not in open contradiction to its basic tenets, and this tendency has been especially apparent in the treatment of deep-rooted popular beliefs. A. Maury points out that the Romans in Celtic areas assimilated Celtic nature-worship. Despite the fact that with the advent of Christianity this nature-worship was constantly denounced, "un respect pieux continuait à entourer les objets si longtemps vénérés; et ce n'était qu'en les consacrant au nouveau culte, qu'en sanctifiant pour ainsi dire les vestiges païens," that the new cult dealt effectively with the more tenacious superstitions. [44] The belief in fairy superna-

---

[42] *Op. cit.*, p. 453.
[43] *White Magic: An Introduction to the Folklore of Christian Legend* (Cambridge, Mass., 1948), 6.
[44] *Croyances et Légendes du Moyen Age* (Paris, 1896), 13.

tural had profound roots; "les fées," says Maury, "nous apparaissent comme le dernier et le plus persistent de tous les vestiges que le paganism a laissés empreints dans les esprits."[45] Thus the fairy supernatural was frequently adapted in a manner consistent with Christian conceptions. MacCulloch in his discussion of "Fairy" notes the two possible evolutions of fairy-belief in contact with Christianity. "Fairies in Christian lands," he reports, "are generally regarded as pagans... The Church was generally opposed to fairies, associating them with paganism, the devil, and witchcraft."[46] On the other hand, "fairyland is sometimes in close association with the Christian Otherworld."[47] He notes too that while the tales of Elysium, the Celtic happy Otherworld, are mainly remouldings of earlier pagan originals, they have "in many ways been influenced by Christian ideas, although their main incidents are purely pagan. In later Celtic tales, the *imrama* or 'Voyages,' Elysium finally is identified with the Christian paradise or Heaven. Pilgrimages replace fairy-lures as reasons for going there."[48]

MacCulloch might have added that fairy-lures are sometimes not replaced, but rather Christianized. In the *Imram Brain* or *Voyage of Bran*, the hero is lured by a magic flowering branch to visit the Otherworld. In 1923 A. C. L. Brown called attention to an Irish version of the voyage of St. Brendan which has a prologue strongly resembling the introductory flower episode of Bran;[49] in this prologue, which differs from previously published versions, the twelve apostles of Ireland saw "a huge, unequalled flower, the conspicuous sign of the Land of Promise," coming toward them "from the glittering Land of Promise, from the King of Kings, from the royal Ruler," and they vow to "seek the land of the flower until they should meet with the secrets of

---

[45] *Ibid.*, p. 30.
[46] J. A. MacCulloch, "Blest, Abode of the (Celtic)," in J. Hastings, ed., *Encyclopaedia of Religion and Ethics*, V (New York, 1912), 680.
[47] *Ibid.*, p. 682. It is of course not surprising, in light of the various conceptions of fairyland which existed, that the fairy Otherworld might be more easily assimilable than fairies themselves to the Christian conceptions.
[48] *Ibid.*, p. 695.
[49] "The Wonderful Flower that Came to St. Brendan," *Manly Anniversary Studies* (Chicago, 1923), 296-99.

God." [50] An Irish incident is worked into a Christian legend, and the fairy Otherworld becomes the land of Promise.

In noting the relation between the *Bran* and *Brendan* accounts, Brown fails to point out a fact which makes their similarity less surprising: that a Christian element already exists in the *Bran* account. The quatrains which the mysterious woman sings in inviting Bran to visit the Otherworld are not limited to a description of the delights to be found there. Rather, they assume the form of a quite obvious prophecy:

> A great birth will come after ages,
> That will not be in a lofty place.
> The son of a woman whose mate will not be known,
> He will seize the rule of the many thousands.
> A rule without beginning, without end,
> He has created the world so that it is perfect,
> Whose are earth and sea,
> Woe to him that shall be under His unwill!
> 'Tis He that made the heavens,
> Happy he that has a white heart.
> He will purify hosts under pure water,
> 'Tis He that will heal your sickness. (quatrains 26-8)

Bran sets out to seek this Otherworld, and during his journey he encounters "a man in a chariot coming towards him over the sea," who reveals that he is Manannan, and sings more quatrains to Bran. Like those of the woman who had visited Bran previously, these quatrains concern first the beauty and happiness of the Otherworld, then assume the tone of prophecy, and their reference to the original Paradise is unmistakable:

> We are from the beginning of creation
> Without old age, without consummation of earth,
> Hence we expect not that there should be frailty,
> The sin has not come to us.
> An evil day when the Serpent went
> To the father to his city!
> She has perverted the times in this world,
> So that there came decay which was not original.
> By greed and lust he has slain us,
> Through which he has ruined his noble race;

---

[50] *Ibid.*, p. 299.

> The withered body has gone to the fold of torment,
> And everlasting abode of torture.
> It is a law of pride in this world
> To believe in the creatures, to forget God,
> Overthrow by diseases, and old age,
> Destruction of the soul through deception.
> A noble salvation will come
> From the King who has created us,
> A white law will come over seas,
> Besides being God, he will be man.   (quatrains 44-8) [51]

These prophetic passages demonstrate that the combination of fairy material with Christian elements existed already in the early stages of recorded Celtic fairy tradition. Alfred Nutt in his study of that tradition explains that after Christianity was introduced into Ireland in the fifth century, in the following three centuries "the main interest of Irish history lies in the efforts of the Irish race to organise Christianity within and propagate it outside Ireland, and in the manifestations of the effect produced upon the Irish world by the revelation of Romano-Greek culture. But stories of the same nature as those told of the pre-Christian kings continue to be told of their Christian successors." [52] He emphasizes that "although these involve, as already stated, marvellous elements to fully as great an extent as in the case of the pre-Christian kings, yet the machinery is nominally Christian, some benefit or injury done to a saint being generally the originating cause of the events narrated in the story," [53] and considers this development so general that he terms these centuries the "Christian legendary period."

---

[51] The discussion of a text such as that of *Bran* is hindered by the fact that readings for parts of even the most basic Old Irish texts have not yet been established. Meyer, for example, translates one quatrain of *Bran* as follows:

> An ancient tree there is with blossoms,
> On which birds call to the Hours.
> 'Tis in harmony it is that their wont
> To call together every Hour. (quatrain 7)

This he interprets as "the canonical hours, an allusion to church music" (*Bran*, I, p. 6), a reference which if correct further demonstrates the penetration of the text by Christian elements. However, Zimmer translates "to the Hours" as "zu der Zeiten" (*loc. cit.*), a reminder that conclusions based on such disputed readings or interpretations are only tentative.

[52] *Op. cit.*, p. 121; for examples, see pp. 122-23.
[53] *Ibid.*, p. 94.

The tale of the voyage of Bran is not the only early Celtic Otherworld tale containing easily identifiable Christian elements. In the *Echtra Condla* too a maiden comes to visit the hero and to invite him to the Otherworld, and in this case Connla's father the King urges his Druids to chant against her, as she is clearly a fairy, visible only to the youth. She answers the King: "Druidism is not loved, little has it progressed to honour on the Great Strand. When his law shall come it will scatter the charms of Druids from journeying on the lips of the black, lying demons." [54] Nutt comments that in both these accounts, of Connla and of Bran, the Christian element produces "the same impression of being thrust into the story without rhyme or reason." [55] Because of such similarities, in Nutt's opinion they must be considered "as products of one school, in which old traditions were handled with a particular spirit and with an evident desire to make them palatable in orthodox eyes." [56]

While the Christian element in these two tales does seem to be included "without rhyme or reason," one point is of great importance for the present study. The Christian element, while it is intruded, is in both tales introduced by the fairy figure, and is associated with the Otherworld to which she urges the hero to come. The fairy is in fact the spokesman and the representative of the Christian tradition in these works. This is a point of some importance, because in later developments of the fairy mythology it was the fairy Otherworld which was most easily assimilated to Christian belief, while the fairy herself was often exiled to the demonic realm. Scholars have long considered that the fairy lore as found in medieval tales is a phenomenon in no way connected with Christian thought, and the awakening of interest in the possibilities of Christian interpretation of medieval secular works is a relatively recent development. It is thus of some interest to note that the Celts, from whom, according to many scholars, the medieval writers derived so much of their Otherworld con-

---

[54] *Ibid.*, p. 146. The maiden refers to the Otherworld as "the lands of the living, where is neither death, nor sin, nor transgression."
[55] *Ibid.*, p. 148.
[56] *Ibid.*, p. 149.

ception and fairy lore, experienced no great difficulty in combining an obvious fairy-mistress story with obvious Christian elements. We should not, then, be entirely surprised by the suggestion that some of the writers of lay and romance might have effected a similar combination, in a form relevant to the Christian emphases of their own period.

Even in the realm of lay and romance itself, we need not seek combinations of fairy-lore and Christian significance in hidden places only. Sometimes they are quite explicit.[57] In the lay *Yonec* by Marie de France, the lament of the imprisoned lady is answered by the appearance of a bird which becomes before her eyes a "chevaler bel et gent" (v. 115). This knight promises to be the ideal lover, thus reassuring the lady who eventually accepts him as her *ami*. Before the relationship is established, however, Marie is careful to assure us that we have here an example of white magic, not black. The lady's lament itself, after referring to stories she had heard of ideal lovers, concludes with an appeal to God:

> Si ceo peot estre e ceo fu,
> Si unc a nul est avenu,
> Deu, ki de tut ad poësté,
> Il en face ma volenté! (vv. 101-104)

It is then that the bird-knight makes his appearance. Lest the reader still doubt as to the nature of the magic, Marie offers conclusive evidence. The lady, as hesitant as the reader to interpret this supernatural occurrence, agrees to accept the knight as her *ami* only on certain conditions: "S'en Deu creïst e issi fust Que lur amur estre peüst" (vv. 139-40). The knight approves her impulse:

> 'Dame,' dit il, 'vus dites bien.
> Ne vodreie pur nule rien
> Que de mei i ait acheisun,
> Mescreaunce u suspesçun.' (vv. 145-148)

---

[57] I am indebted to Dr. U. T. Holmes for pointing out to me the frequent relevance of the concepts of black and white magic to the fairy elements in lay and romance.

He affirms his Christian belief, and verifies it by taking the Sacrament, thus fully convincing the lady. Furthermore, it is not only in the introduction to the story that Marie is concerned to assert God's approval, for when, long after the knight's death, the lady, her husband, and her son are mysteriously guided to the abbey where her lover is still honored and where his son is awaited, she cries out to the boy:

'Beaus fiz,' fet ele, 'avez oï
Cum Deus nus ad mené ici...' (vv. 527-28)

Passing from lay to romance, we again find evidence that the presentation of guarantees of Christianity in an amorous fairy-mortal relationship was not foreign to the imagination of medieval authors. There are several well-known romances in which the fairy, like the knight in Marie's poem, asserts Christian belief. Mélior, after explaining to her chosen future mate Partonopeus that she has guided his adventures to lead him to her, explains that she is a Christian. Morgan the Fay in her role as mistress of Ogier le Danois is at first mistaken by the hero to be the Virgin; when, after two hundred years of enjoying the hero's company, she sees that Christianity is clearly endangered, she sends him back to the world of mortals to combat the foes of the Faith, after which he returns to his fairy mistress. In the late *chanson de geste* of *Maugis d'Aigrement*, the fay Oriande when she happens upon an abandoned child prays that God will make his origin known. This information is furnished by a magician, and Oriande prays to God to preserve the child, then takes him with her and has him baptized. Having thus provided for his Christian well-being, she shows her fairy colors by arranging for his education in necromancy.

A. Maury cites another example of this Christianization of the fairy lover, that of Melusine's assurance to Raimondin. In Maury's opinion the "origine païenne des fées explique les sentiments d'animadversion qu'on leur prête contre le christianisme, cette défiance que leur foi inspire même aux mortels qui sont épris de leurs charmes." As the Church generally tended to account for the fairy magic of popular belief as witchcraft, "une sorte d'opposition s'établit naturellement entre la Vierge et les fées, comme entre

Dieu et le démon, et, par une sorte d'expiation, le christianisme substitua des idées, empruntées à sa foi, à celles que le paganisme avait accréditées. Sous cette influence, les fées ont souvent fait place à la Vierge. En Suisse, les trois fées sont devenues les Trois Maries..."[58] We have seen that this confusion is not limited to folklore, appearing also in literary form, as when Ogier mistakes Morgain for the Virgin. Another example is found in the romance of *Rigomer*,[59] in which Lancelot, wounded in terrible combat, falls as dead, but is immediately healed by the ointment of a mysterious damsel dressed in white. The amazed witnesses of this healing can only imagine that the damsel is accomplishing a Christian miracle:

> 'Cist est garis a poi de paine!
> C'est ci Marie Madelaine,
> S'a aporté de l'ongement
> Dont ele fist a Diu present!
> Auquant jurent Saint Bertemiu;
> 'Ains est la viele mere Diu,
> Car autre n'en peüst finer!

All their guesses are wrong, however, for as the author of the poem tells us,

> Ne sevent nient adeviner,
> Car ce fu ma dame Lorie,
> Li mon segnor Gauvain amie.

One other type of combination of the pagan and Christian supernatural has been found less difficult to accept and to explain: that found in medieval legends concerning the lives of saints. We have seen early examples of this in the development of the Celtic *imrama*, a development which found its culmination in the *Voyage of Saint Brandan*. This very famous tale, says Nutt, "is but the latest and a definitely Christian example of a *genre* of story-telling which had already flourished for centuries in Ireland when it seemed good to an unknown writer to dress the old half-Pagan

---

[58] *Op. cit.*, pp. 34-5.
[59] "Rigomer," *Histoire littéraire de la France*, xxx, 93.

marvels in orthodox monkish garb, and thus start them afresh on their triumphal march through the literature of the world." [60]

Some Celticists have attempted to use this evidence of syncretism of Christian and pagan ideas in the *imrama* and other Celtic sources as proof of Celtic provenance of various elements of Arthurian tradition. A. C. L. Brown refers to Nutt's explanation of the Grail as the development and Christianization of the Celtic vessel of plenty, and asserts that the transition from a fairy-abode with its cauldron of plenty to the Church with food supplied by angels is traced in the *imrama*. The history of the St. Brendan legend, according to Brown's analysis, shows the same sort of development as that of the Grail. The Christianization of pagan deities and pagan marvels, he says, "is believed to have been especially prevalent in Ireland, where the first missionaries showed a generous indulgence toward such popular beliefs as were not positively inimical to Christianity, and where monks copied down and preserved stories of the older pagan time." [61]

Maury in his study of the pious legends points out that the saint stories are patterned naturally on the life of Christ, or those of female saints frequently on that of Marie, with borrowings from the Old Testament also. There may be other prototypes. [62] H. Newstead contends that in Wales "the originally divine nature of Bran was assimilated to Christian tradition, just as the magic possessions of Celtic sea gods were naturally identified with the sacred objects in Christian ritual and as legends of other pagan gods and heroes filtered into the biographies of saints... In view of the medieval tendency toward syncretism, there is nothing astonishing in the attempt to adapt the pagan legend of Bran to Christian hagiography." [63] This process, as Maury points out, was applied to other personages in addition to the saints: "Cette imitation de la Bible se retrouve encore, quoique rarement, dans la vie des personages célèbres qui n'ont point un caractère spécial de sainteté. D'où cela provient-il? C'est que dans les premiers siècles de barbarie il y avait infiniment moins de distance qu'aujourd'hui

---

[60] *Op. cit.*, p. 161.
[61] "From Cauldron of Plenty to Grail," *MP*, XIV (1916), 386.
[62] *Op. cit.*, p. 130.
[63] *Bran the Blessed*, pp. 44-45.

entre l'illustration sacrée et l'illustration politique et guerrière... Dans les idées du moyen âge, il existe entre Dieu et l'univers une véritable solidarité. Partout où il y a succès et triomphe, vertus et puissance, là est la divinité qui agit et protège, qui manifeste sa présence par des prodiges." [64]

These two types of combination of Christian and pagan supernatural, that found in the saints' legends and that found in the lays and romances, in fact are based on a single general operative principle involved in the term "magic." C. Grant Loomis in his work on white magic notes that the common factor in all conceptions of magic is that magic deals in wares of an unnatural kind. "Magic is a practise which seeks to turn events or to control nature in an unnatural and unexpected fashion... suggests aid from sources lying in the unseen and in the unknown; it is a secret mastering influence which inspires wonder or fear." [65] The essential point to retain in considering the medieval treatment of material involving magic, of the supernatural of whatever type, is that magic "is neither good nor evil in itself, for of itself it has no will;" it is rarely conceived as a separate and impartial force, as the use of its power "depends wholly upon the will of the agent." [66] Loomis attempts to describe the deep roots of the interest in magic. "The battle goes on," he says, "between the two worlds of darkness and of light. The means or the interpretation of the means have changed their symbols and some of their terms." [67] Christianity in this regard incorporated a fund of common lore that is older than itself; "the lore of wonder lived among the people. Their belief in a cult of heroes and supernatural men, coupled with a multitude of old religious formulas and superstitions, had a continuous tradition. Theoretical theology was forced to recognize the impossibility of stamping out the belief in magic. A wise substitution of Christian magical elements was made wherever possible. Old beliefs were reinterpreted and the cult of wonder served to capture the popular imagination." [68]

---

[64] *Op. cit.*, p. 130.
[65] *Op. cit.*, p. 3.
[66] *Loc. cit.*
[67] *Ibid.*, p. 6.
[68] *Ibid.*, p. 110.

The evidences here assembled of the mingling of Christian and pagan supernatural generally deal with phenomena which took place as part of the early development of a mythic conception itself, or which more or less obviously attempted to combine the two on the surface level of a story. Examples of the latter include the Christian sections of the Bran and Connla stories, which were perhaps interpolations, and the professions of faith of various fairy lovers who claim to represent a good, not an evil, manifestation of the supernatural. In none of these do we find an author systematically applying a Christian concept to a fairy frame-tale with the intent of utilizing the fairy-story interest in the service of a larger conception. Examples of this will be suggested in the following chapter, in connection with symbolic interpretation of medieval works; here it suffices to note that fairy-Christian combinations of elements were not unknown, and apparently not repugnant, to medieval thought.

What is the importance of the Otherworld concept in the lay of *Guingamor*? Comparison of the poem with other lays which relate a mortal's connection with a fay and a resulting contact with the Otherworld reveal that the proportion of Otherworld to this-world material is much greater in *Guingamor* than in *Guigemar, Lanval,* or *Graelent*. In *Guingamor* a large part of the action takes place in the Otherworld. In this lay of 674 verses, the entry of the hero into the Otherworld begins with the dawn of his day of *aventure*, in v. 248. The boar-hunt which leads him into the forest gets under way in v. 269, and Guingamor actually penetrates into the forest at v. 300. If we are to attach any importance to the poet's relative weighting of elements, we must conclude that the Otherworld adventure was his principal interest, and that the material preceding it was handled in such a way as to lead into this adventure as quickly as possible.[69]

---

[69] Among the most common elements of the references to this hero in medieval works other than the lay is a connection of him with the Otherworld, sometimes with an Otherworld isle in general, sometimes specifically with Avalon. Chrétien in the *Erec* tells us that "De l'isle d'Avalons fu sire" (v. 1905); Brangemuer, according to Wauchier, "Rois fu des illes de la mer" (v. 21, 876), a position which he presumably inherited from his father Guingamor, who had enjoyed it because of his relation to Brangemuer's mother the fay. Dame Liones' brother Gryngamor lives in the "yle of Avylyon" (Malory, ch. 26).

How does this visit to the Otherworld, which the poet apparently seeks to stress, represent the tradition of such voyages, and how does it differ from that tradition? The study of the two aspects of Otherworld and voyage as found in the early Irish tales resulted in the identification of the following general elements: the Otherworld is a place where one may enjoy both "simple sensuous pleasures" and deathlessness; it is a place difficult of access, which only specially chosen or privileged mortals may visit; and after one has entered and enjoyed the life there, return to the mortal world is perilous, if not impossible. The Welsh Otherworld conception is apparently quite similar, with interest focused on the marvellous nature of the beauty and delights experienced. The Faërie of lay and romance, although in some ways resembling the Celtic Otherworld, is in fact quite different, having no specific characteristics other than the marvellous, and these characteristics being dependent on the reasons for existence of a particular manifestation of the fairy supernatural. A more specific Arthurian Otherworld, Avalon, is sometimes identified with Faërie, but usually associated with the legend of Arthur, his healing, and his expected return.

It is clear from this summary that the Otherworld concept is complex, and it is necessary to disentangle the threads of the Otherworld visit of Guingamor in order to determine the relation of the lay to the Otherworld-voyage tradition.

Our point of departure is the point of the hero's entry into the Otherworld. He who visits the Otherworld of Faërie is generally chosen, although he is frequently not aware of the fact until much later. He is drawn to the Otherworld by the fay, who has chosen him for her *ami*, and her fairy influence guides his actions until he reaches her side. In *Guingamor*, however, this particular element of the hero's visit to Faërie does not function. If the knight is drawn into the forest through the influence of the fay, we are told nothing of it, although the fairy has every opportunity to confess her influence if it has in fact been operative, and comparison with other tales indicates that the traditional fairy is not likely to be hesitant to do so. On the contrary, the boar-hunt which leads Guingamor into the Otherworld is occasioned by the vengeful challenge of the spurned queen, who knows the hunt to be dangerous (as ten of the best knights have been "lost" while engaged in it) and hopes by this means to rid herself of the knight whose presence has become not only unbearable to her but also potentially dangerous.

One detail remains puzzling if we accept this explanation of Guingamor's entry into the Otherworld: that of the knight's acceptance of the Queen's implied challenge. The poet tells us that Guingamor "a bien entendu Qu'elle a por lui cest plet meu" (vv. 165-66). As noted in the preceding chapter, the scholars who have studied the lay, unable to account for this reaction of the knight, have generally resorted to the explanation that actually all of this prelude to the boar-hunt is being controlled by the fairy, in the same way that the Ile d'Or maiden in the *Biaus Desconeüs* is responsible for the damsel who appeared at Arthur's court requesting aid, the fay knowing that her chosen hero will be the one to respond. These scholars decide that Guingamor's acceptance of the challenge is of this type, due to the fairy influence, although he is himself quite unaware of any such possibility.

There is only one objection to be made to this interpretation, but its seriousness entitles us to ask whether some other explanation may not be possible. The interpretation, entirely plausible in terms of the fairy-mistress tradition, is unfortunately not borne out by any evidence from the lay itself. It is therefore perhaps of interest for its suggestion that *Guingamor* does belong to a larger tradition, but it is of no value in a consideration of the unique literary manifestation, the lay in its extant form.

If we seek some other explanation, what alternatives confront us? Taking the challenge at its face value, we might suppose that Guingamor, realizing that the queen is trying to be rid of him (as he must realize, for her suggestion of the hunt is seen by him as a "plet"), is convinced that due to the delicacy of the situation he had best comply. This posible explanation is contradicted, however, by the fact that the knight is filled with joy at the prospect of undertaking the *aventure*. If the hunt were considered to be as dangerous as the king indicates, and an undertaking which the knight himself recognizes as designed to lead to his destruction as it had presumably led to that of ten valiant knights before him, his exaltation is difficult to explain. He is the only one of the entire assembly (with the possible exception of the queen) to feel joy. The king grieves, while the queen is relieved to be rid of him —"Delivrée en cuide estre atant, Nel verra mes en son vivant" (vv. 241-42). But after the king at the urging of the queen grants his prize dog and horse for the hunt, Guingamor takes his leave and "a son ostel liez s'en alla" (v. 246). Even the townspeople are aware of the great danger of the hunt as they escort him out of the town: "o grant dolor et o grant cri ... Merveilleus duel por lui faisoient" (vv. 266, 268), but Guingamor does not seem to share their apprehension. The queen's indirect challenge has been pronounced, the poet tells us, "por lui grever et corroucier" (v. 149); the result, however, is not anger, but rather eagerness and joy. Guingamor does accept the challenge, but his reaction indicates that it has an appeal for him of a positive kind, and represents more than mere negative obedience to an implied command from the angered wife of his king.

We have now tentatively eliminated two possible explanations for Guingamor's acceptance of the challenge, that of fairy influence and that of simple obedience to the queen's implied command. Is there another possibility? A clue may be found in the early Celtic Otherworld tales. To both the Celtic Otherworld and Faërie, the hero receives a special summons. The summons to Faërie as found in the fairy-mistress tale is typically by, or occasioned by, a fay, who is drawing the hero to the Otherworld for her own purposes. In the Celtic Otherworld inductions, the appeal which is made to the hero is frequently in terms of special qualities of the Otherworld, such as the deathlessness enjoyed there, and the hero is specifically chosen to make the voyage. We find in the invitation to Bran cited above a curious parallel to our puzzling element in *Guingamor*. The mysterious woman who comes to invite the hero reveals that he alone is in some way especially qualified to understand the summons of the Otherworld:

> Not to all of you is my speech,
> Though its great marvel has been made known;
> Let Bran hear from the crown of the world
> What of wisdom has been told to him. (quatrain 29)

It is Bran who will respond to the appeal of the Otherworld, although the "great marvel" has been made known to all his companions. In *Guingamor* a mysterious pursuit has been named as a challenge in the presence of the king's assembled company of knights, and Guingamor for some reason knows that it is relevant to him alone. What this reason may be, will be discussed in the following chapter.

The Otherworld which Guingamor enters in pursuit of the boar is in its appearance that of Faërie. Its "lande aventureuse" and "riviere perilleuse" are those of the romances; the knight enters into "une lande" and sees "une clere fonteloie," and when he penetrates deep into the forest he happens upon a strange "palès." When he enters this he finds it uninhabited, and gazes with awe upon its riches —its green marble, its gold and silver, its doors of "fin yvoire," the "merveilleuse clarté" about it. There are a number of castles in the romance material which closely resemble this mysterious palace in *Guingamor*, and a number of instances in which the hero, entering such a place, finds it apparently uninhabited. *Partonopeus de Blois* provides a parallel to *Guingamor* with regard to this element, as to numerous others. Schofield noted that it is "common enough" in medieval romances, and is found several times in the story of Perceval, with three distinct cases in the *Conte del Graal*.[70] Newstead indicates the similarity of both *Guingamor* and *Partonopeus* to one of the four traditional tales of the *Mabinogion*, that of *Manawydan mab Llyr*. In this Welsh adventure Pryderi and his father are pursuing a white boar, and come to a castle where one had never been seen before; Pryderi investigates, and inside he finds "neither man nor beast."[71] The same author points out an interesting episode of an apparently uninhabited castle found in the Bran de Lis section of Pseudo-Wauchier's *Graal* continuation. Gawain, seeking lodging for Arthur and his party of knights, "sees a fair castle on the bank of a broad river. Beside a fountain by the bridge he finds two maidens... After greeting them he rides over the bridge into the castle and marvels at the wealth displayed in the streets —rich vessels, coins, costly stuffs. But no one is visible. Within the hall tables are richly set with food, though no living soul appears...he

---

[70] "Guingamor," p. 225.
[71] "Partonopeus," p. 922.

returns to the bridge to speak to the maidens, 'les pucieles qui samblent fees,' but even they have vanished." [72]

The actual description of the palace found by Guingamor is traced by Hoepffner to two lays of Marie, *Yonec* and *Guigemar*. The doors of the city of Muldumarec, like those of *Guingamor*'s palace, are wide open, and there is no barrier to entry; within the city, as within the palace, "Home ne fame n'i trova" (*Yonec* vv. 379-80). [73] These elements "sont complétées par quelques détails fournis par *Guigemar*... au lieu d'un château, c'est d'abord une nef magique que rencontre Guigemar. Le vaisseau est, comme le château, d'une richesse inouïe," while the bed found on the enchanted boat is, Hoepffner asserts, the model for the doors of the palace in *Guingamor*; the doors are "de fin yvoire, D'or entaillies a trifoire" (vv. 369-700), and the bed "taillié a or, tot a trifoire, De ciprès et de blanc ivoire" (vv. 173-74). A castle too is found in *Guigemar*, at the end of the wounded knight's voyage, and "c'est lui qui a fourni le marbre vert des murailles" of the *Guingamor* palace. [74] Whatever the specific derivations of its elements, this "palès" is essentially a commonplace of tales of this type.

When Guingamor returns to the palace, having accepted the fay's invitation, he finds it now filled with three hundred knights or more, each richly dressed and accompanied by his *amie*.

> Molt ert bele la compaingnie;
> Vallez i ot a espreviers,
> O biaus ostors fors et muiers;
> El pales en ot autretant,
> As tables, as esches jouant. (vv. 514-18)

There are other delights which, as we have seen, were already characteristic of the Otherworld in the early Celtic tales:

> Molt fu la nuit bien herbergiez,
> Bons mengiers ot a grant plenté,
> O grant deduit, o grant fierté,

---

[72] *Bran the Blessed*, pp. 70-71.
[73] E. Hoepffner, "Marie de France et les Lais Anonymes," *Studi Medievali*, N. S. 4 (1931), 5.
[74] *Ibid.*, p. 6.

> Sons de herpes et de vieles,
> Chanz de vallez et de puceles;
> Grant merveille ot de la noblece,
> De la beauté, de la richesce. (vv. 526-32)

Similar descriptions are found in other romances. In both the Castle of Maidens and the *Castiel Orguellous*, as in fact in the *Val sans Retor*, each knight enjoys the company of an *amie* and a life of infinite delight.

Schofield says that *Guingamor* is similar to all the other tales of its type in that in it "a valiant mortal finds his way unexpectedly to the other world, where he is kept a willing but unwitting prisoner by a fascinating woman for a very long (though apparently very short) term of years, sustained by supernatural food and enjoying marvellous pleasures." [75] However, as previously pointed out, in *Guingamor* there is no indication of a retention or imprisonment. In the frequent examples of fairy-retention tales the device which induces the hero to remain is usually made quite clear and is an important element in the story. For example, in the *Livre d'Artus*, P. the Queen of Danemark is holding prisoner in the Castle of Maidens various knights of Arthur. "As each knight entered, a *pucele* offered him an apple, and if he ate, he lost all desire and power to leave, for he found in the garden all the delights of the world." [76] Even our hero's counterpart Guiomar was retained by Morgain in joyful idleness in the *Val sans Retor*. But no such device is described in *Guingamor*; the hero, if we are to judge by what our author tells us rather than by what we expect him to tell us, eats no fairy food, falls under no fairy spell. He is invited to stay, is promised the boar which is the object of his quest, is attracted to the fay, and accepts her invitation.

What, then, of the fact that Guingamor, who "N'i cuida que deus jors ester, Et au tierz s'en cuida raler" (vv. 532-33), finds when he seeks to leave that three hundred years have passed as three days? Does this supernatural passing of time indicate a fairy "captivity?"

---

[75] "Guingamor," p. 227.
[76] Loomis, *Arthurian Tradition*, p. 113.

The idea of the supernatural passing of time in the Otherworld is one found in early Celtic Otherworld tales such as the *Voyage of Bran*, in which the hero and his companions visit the Land of Women, where "it seemed a year to them that they were there —it chanced to be many years." [77] And it must have been many years indeed, for when the voyagers approach Ireland and are asked who they are, and Bran replies that he is Bran son of Febal, he receives from the questioner the reply that "we do not know such a one, though the Voyage of Bran is in our ancient stories." [78] Newstead points out that the motif of suspended time in the Otherworld is not foreign to early Welsh tales: in the episode called the "Hospitality of the Noble Head" in the story of Bran the Blessed, the participants spend eighty years in a "fair and royal place," in such delights that "they were unconscious of having ever spent a time more joyous and mirthful than it. Nor did one of them know of the other that he was older by that time when they came there." [79]

In these Celtic tales of the supernatural passage of time in the Otherworld the phenomenon is apparently due to the nature of the Otherworld itself, rather than to a specific enchantment designed to keep mortals there. Furthermore, in these tales it is considered a *positive* element of the Otherworld, connected with the absence of aging. We recall that the joyful inhabitants of the Otherworld described to Bran are "without grief, without sorrow, without death, Without any sickness, without debility..." (quatrain 10), and that the damsel who invites Connla to the Otherworld urges him to leave his mortal companions because " 'Tis no lofty seat on which Connla sits among short-lived companions awaiting fearful death." [80]

This presentation of the supernatural passage of time is altered when it is made a fairy-device for the retention of heroes. MacCulloch says that fairies have the power of "putting a spell upon mortals which holds them bound for long periods of time," and that the fairy glamour corresponds "with their power of making

---

[77] *Bran*, p. 30 (section 62).
[78] *Ibid.*, p. 32 (section 64).
[79] *Bran the Blessed*, p. 16.
[80] Nutt, p. 128.

time appear long or short to those mortals who are lured into their company." [81] Child outlines the story of Ogier, who is drawn to Avalon by Morgan the Fay. "She puts a ring on his finger which restores his youth, and then places a crown on his head which makes him forget all the past. For two hundred years Ogier lived in such delights as no worldly being can imagine, and the two hundred years seemed to him but twenty." [82] Even when Ogier, having returned to France to defend Christianity, wearies of his mortal life and attempts to leave it by casting into the fire the firebrand given him as a token of continued youth, instantly becoming an old man of three hundred years, the fairy will not let his destiny escape her control:

> Ainsi le corps Ogier ille se declinoit
> Et ainsi que le bers en ce peril estoit
> Y vint Morgue la fee qui le danois amoit
> Et osta le tison qui ens ou feu flamboit
> Dedens un riche char qui tout de feu sembloit
> Fist eslever Ogier et si le ravissoit
> Et ne seut qu'il devint labbe qui la estoit
> Ensement fu ravis en faerie droit. [83]

Hofer, acknowledging that this motif at least the author of *Guingamor* appears not to have drawn from Marie, notes the possibility of derivation from such tales as *Bran* and suggests another possible influence, that of the medieval Christian tradition which provides similar accounts. Among these "zu nennen wäre in diesem Zusammenhang ausser der Legende von den Sept Dormanz auch die Erzählung des 1196 gestorbenen Maurice de Sully ... Und ist nicht im Psalmvers die gleiche Voraussetzung eingeschlossen, wenn es heisst: 'Unus dies apud Deum sicut mille anni et mille anni sicut dies unus' (*Seconda epistula Petri*, 3, 8)? Dazu tritt die Stelle in den Psalmen: Quoniam mille anni ante oculos tuos, tamquam dies hesterna, quae praeteriit, et custodia in nocte, quae pro nihilo habentur, eorum anni erunt (*Oratio Moysi hominis Dei* LXXIX, 4)." [84]

---

[81] "Fairy," p. 679.
[82] Quoted in Paton, p. 76.
[83] Quoted in *ibid.*, p. 78.
[84] S. Hofer, "Kritische Bemerkungen zum Lai de Guingamor," *RF*, LXV (1954), 373.

This suggestion raises an interesting point. We have noted in our discussion of the Celtic Otherworld or Elysium that it finally became identified, in the later *imrama*, with the Christian Paradise, and that even earlier, in tales such as *Bran* and *Connla*, the Otherworld was assigned moral qualities strongly reminiscent of the Christian conception. One of the prophetic references in *Bran* is clearly to man before the Fall:

> We are from the beginning of creation
> Without old age, without consummation of earth,
> Hence we expect not that there should be frailty,
> The sin has not come to us. (quatrain 44)

Here the absence of sin is combined with the absence of aging. The same combination is found in *Connla*, where the damsel invites the hero to "the lands of the living, where is neither death, nor sin, nor transgression."[85] In the light of such early combinations of Christian and pagan material, it is appropriate to inquire whether any particular version of the supernatural passing of time may not reflect the earlier Otherworld concept rather than that of Faërie; in other words, whether it may not involve agelessness rather than "retention" or enchantment as its emphasized characteristic. Whether or not one attempts to identify the concept of the supernatural passing of time with Biblical references to time as relative to man and to God, it is certain that the Christian conception at least provides a possible alternate explanation of the occurrence of that phenomenon in a given work.

Guingamor's leave-taking of the Otherworld and his possible return to it, which have been discussed in connection with the fairy-mistress tale, seem also not to conform to the pattern of typical visits by heroes to Faërie. The results of the leave-taking, as well as the warning given the knight by his *amie* before his return to the mortal world, resemble more the early Celtic tales than the typical fairy examples. Because the fay does not seem to control the hero's destiny —as is apparent from the fact that she was not responsible for his entry into the Otherworld, as well as from the type of warning which she gives him— some scholars

---

[85] Nutt, p. 145.

have suggested that the author of *Guingamor* simply borrowed elements from two separate and equally well-known traditions, those of the fairy mistress and the Otherworld voyage, and combined them in a composite work which retains none of the unity of interest of either type of tale. We have seen, however, that not every possibility of a unifying conception has been explored.

Chapter III

GUINGAMOR: AN INTERPRETATION

We have seen that the usual scholarly approaches to the lay of *Guingamor*, explanations of it in terms of its representation of the fairy-mistress or the Otherworld-voyage traditions, have not been completely successful in accounting for a number of distinct elements. They have been even less successful in dealing with the lay as a whole. Unable to detect a unifying conception, scholars studying the poem have almost unanimously assumed that such a conception was not to be found, and they have consequently blamed the anonymous poet for his ineptitude, charging that he handled his traditional materials badly in an unsuccessful attempt to combine two types of tales. Before passing a final judgment on the *Guingamor*-poet and his lay, however, we should return to those questions which have occasioned so much scholarly puzzlement, and inquire whether such criticism has not perhaps mistaken the poet's intent, accusing him of doing badly something which he was not doing at all.

The questions to which satisfactory answers have not been found all concern deviations from the typical fairy-mistress or Otherworld-voyage tales, and the problem is somewhat clarified by listing them in their proper order as they arise in the poem. From such a listing it is apparent that they group naturally about four fundamental problems of interpretation:

I. Why does the lay begin with the "Potiphar's wife" episode? Is this episode related to the rest of the poem?

II. Why does the queen choose the particular device of the boar-hunt as her attempt to rid herself of the knight? Why does

Guingamor know that this is a trap for him, and why does he accept? Why is he "liez" about such a dangerous undertaking?

III. Why does the knight not forget all else when he encounters the fay? Why does she address him in a rather unusual way, and why does he at first decline her invitation? Why does she tell him that he can have the boar only with her aid —and why is this true? What are we to assume about the nature of this Otherworld with its supernatural passage of time and its life of delight?

IV. When Guingamor determines to return to the world of mortals, why does the fay offer a warning about eating and drinking there? What is the significance of the apple-eating and aging episode? Why are the fay's attendants who come for Guingamor not angry, and why do they not leave him for a time to suffer and repent his disobedience? What are we to suppose will be the fate of Guingamor?

It is apparent from the number of these questions and their variety that the text is riddled with elements which are puzzling in terms of traditional considerations of the lay. This may, of course, indicate that the author was indeed unable to control his material; that, borrowing freely from tradition like most of his medieval counterparts, he borrowed almost at random, and was then unable to reconcile the resulting elements. It is possible, however, that such a large number of elements which resist traditional interpretation may indicate that the poet in fact intended something other than an interesting representation of the tradition. Henry Savage raised a similar question concerning the hunting scenes in the English *Gawain and the Green Knight*, and came to the following conclusion: "The question as to whether the order of the hunting scenes in *Gawain* is the result of mere chance grouping or of design on the part of the author can receive, in all probability, no definitive answer. Yet where so much depends upon the nice adjustment of part to part, upon the fusion of separate incidents into unity, and upon the 'dovetailing' together of elements that are diverse, one is inclined to see purpose rather than accident. For Art is the creation not of chance, but of design." [1]

---

[1] Henry L. Savage, "The Significance of the Hunting Scenes in *Gawain and the Green Knight*," *Journal of English and Germanic Philology*, XXVII (1928), 14-15.

It is precisely the "fusion of separate incidents" which is in question in *Guingamor*. Let us give the poet temporary benefit of the doubt. If, in considering each of these puzzling questions in turn, we find some suggestion of a connection to others of the questions, we may suspect that a "dovetailing" of elements is present which is not obvious to the modern reader at first glance, and that something more than coincidence is at work. We must not be too quick to assert that what we do not understand, has no function. [2]

I. The Potiphar's-Wife Incident

This incident is, as previously noted, based on an extremely widespread story. F. E. Faverty, who studied the Potiphar's-wife tale and its complete and partial analogues in medieval literature, considered a complete analogue to be one in which the rejected woman attempts to secure revenge by means of a false accusation. He points out that in the partial analogues, among which he includes *Guingamor's* introductory incident, the "revenge she takes may differ in each case according to the ingenuity of the author. Always, however, the path of innocence is plentifully sprinkled with briars and stones; and always the hero emerges victorious, to the discomfiture of his temptress and the glory of whatever god he happens to be serving." [3] These last words bring to mind the situation presented by the Biblical story itself: Joseph, who is being tested, is the servant of God, and his virtue is under direct attack. In many later examples of this motif, especially in those most relevant to *Guingamor*, the "god" which the hero happens to be serving is an ideal of perfect knightly behavior: one must not betray one's king by responding to the queen's advances. The

---

[2] We must also bear in mind, as Sister M. Amelia Klenke points out concerning Chrétien's *Perceval* (in Urban T. Holmes, Jr. and Sister M. Amelia Klenke, O. P., *Chrétien, Troyes, and the Grail*, Chapel Hill, 1959, p. 195), that "it is not necessary, however possible, that every character and every stage prop had a symbolic meaning. After all, Chrétien was not writing for a research-minded audience."

[3] "The Story of Joseph and Potiphar's Wife in Medieval Literature," (*Harvard*) *Studies and Notes in Philology and Literature*, XIII (1931), 80.

ideal generally arises, and remains, within the social and courtly sphere, and the knight's obedience to his ideal is rewarded, for example in *Lanval* and in *Graelent,* by the love of a damsel fairer than the lofty lady whom he has necessarily rejected; his virtue and his choice are eventually acknowledged by the court society which is their immediate frame of reference. Lanval is dramatically vindicated before the assembled court when his lady appears and is judged most beautiful; Graelent too is freed of suspicion.

Scholars have generally considered that Guingamor's refusal of the queen's advances is identical in its motivation to that of Lanval. When Guingamor says

> Bien sai, dame qu'amer vos doi:
> Fame estes mon seignor le roi,
> Et si vos doi porter honnor
> Comme a la fame mon seignor, (vv. 95-98)

Hofer asserts that "diese Antwort geht auf die Verse 273-76 des 'Lanval' zurück, wenn dort der Befragte betont

> Lungement ai servi le rei
> ne li vueil pas mentir ma fei
> Ja pur vus ne pur vostre amur
> ne mesferai a mun seignur!" [4]

Faverty too says that when the queen offers the knight her love, "being loyal to the king, he indignantly refuses her and leaves the room." [5] However, the replies of Guingamor and of Lanval are not identical, either in tone or in content.

The queen has summoned Guingamor to her side, and speaks first:

> 'Guingamor, molt estes vaillans,
> Preuz et cortois et avenans:
> Riche aventure vos atent;
> Amer pouez molt hautement.
> Amie avez cortoise et bele:
> Je ne sai dame ne danzele

---

[4] *Op. cit.,* p. 367.
[5] *Op. cit.,* p. 98.

> El roiaume de sa valor,
> Si vos aimme de grant amor:
> Bien la tenez por vostre drue.'
> Li chevaliers l'a respondue:
> 'Dame,' fet il, 'ne sai comment
> J'amasse dame durement,
> S'ançois ne l'eusse veue
> Et acointie et conneue:
> Onques mes n'en oi parler;
> Ne quier ouan d'amor ovrer.'
> La roine li dist: 'Amis,
> Ne soiez mie si eschis:
> Moi devez vos trés bien amer;
> Je ne faz mie à refuser,
> Car je vos aim de bon corage
> Et amerai tout mon aage.'
> Li chevaliers s'est porpensez,
> Si respondi comme senez:
> 'Bien sai, dame, qu'amer vos doi:
> Fame estes mon seignor le roi,
> Et si vos doi porter honnor
> Comme a la fame mon seignor.'
> La roine li respondi:
> 'Je ne di mie amer ainsi:
> Amer vos voil de druerie,
> Et que je soie vostre amie.
> Vos estes biax et je sui gente:
> S'a moi amer metez entente,
> Molt poons estre andui hetié.'
> Vers lui le tret, si l'a besié. (vv. 71-106)

Of great importance is the manner in which the motif is actually incorporated into *Guingamor*. In the first place, the queen's declaration of love is not abrupt. She approaches the youth gently, attempting to make him lower his guard. She does not mention herself in her opening remarks, but instead flatters him and tells him that he has for his love the fairest and most worthy damsel of the kingdom. Guingamor replies that the situation which she describes is quite impossible, as he knows no such damsel, and in addition is not at present concerned about love. The queen becomes bold, and reproaches his obliqueness —"Ne soiez mie si eschis," she urges impatiently. She then tells him that he should love her well, as she loves him, and again he replies with a manoeuvre. We know that this move on his part is deliberate, for the poet tells us that "li chevaliers s'est porpensez, Si respondi comme senez." Instead of brutally rejecting her love, in the manner of Lanval, Guingamor attempts to leave an honorable retreat for the queen by pretending to misunderstand the type of love she requires of him. It is at this point that the queen, unable to restrain herself and exasperated by the knight's skill in parrying her verbal thrusts, makes her intentions quite clear. Guingamor now has no choice; the harm is done. Still he does not make harsh reply, like Lanval; rather, he feels great shame, and attempts to leave her. She seizes him by the cloak, tearing it so that it remains in her hands while he hastens from the room.

Examination of this scene reveals that in several ways it differs from other instances of the motif in the romance material. In *Lanval* and in *Graelent*, for example, the situation itself, the motif, is all-important: the queen offers herself to a virtuous young knight, who refuses her. The incident in *Guingamor*, however, contains and emphasizes additional elements. The first of these is the actual dialogue between the queen and Guingamor, a matching of wits and of qualities which is not present in the rather abrupt encounters of *Lanval* and *Graelent*.

A second element, the seizure of the knight's mantle, has been a source of puzzlement. As Guingamor is leaving, the queen grasps the garment, which tears and remains in her hands. This element is not generally found in the medieval literary versions, and scholars have decided that it should not be found in *Guingamor*. Schofield, who in his early study of the lay recognized the introductory situation as a Potiphar's-wife episode, uses this mantle element as support for his contention that the inclusion of the motif in the lay is unjustified and badly incorporated. "Observe in particular," he says, "that the queen grasps Guingamor's mantle when he is leaving her in righteous indignation. In the poem, however, the point of the incident is lost. The queen, unlike Potiphar's wife, makes no use of the mantle. She simply returns it by a messenger." [6] Hoepffner too feels that the detail is extraneous: "Il y a dans Guingamor un détail étrange et complètement

---

[6] "Guingamor," p. 238.

inutile: le chavelier, en fuyant, laisse son manteau entre les mains de la reine et celle-ci le lui fait remettre, sans qu'il s'en aperçoive. A notre avis ce n'est pas, comme on l'a prétendu, pour remplacer les cadeaux que la dame amoureuse envoyait à son chevalier; l'auteur s'est simplement souvenu de l'histoire célèbre de Joseph et de la femme de Potiphar qu'il a gauchement exploitée ici." [7]

Only one serious critical attempt has been made to explain the inclusion of this particular detail in the poem. S. Foster Damon, considering *Guingamor* to be by Marie, uses it as an example of the special treatment of love which he believes to be characteristic of the technique of the poetess. He recognizes that the situation is a stock one, and attempts to demonstrate the uniqueness of the author's handling: "The queen, having caught at Guingamor, is left holding his cloak. She has evidence which she can use against him, in true Biblical fashion." Damon then protests Schofield's contention quoted above that the point of the incident is lost in the lay because the queen makes no use of the mantle: "But is the point lost? Is it not rather that the queen here is deliberately contrasted to the wife in *Genesis*? Is she not a lady, terrified at her act, and getting rid of the incriminating evidence, without one thought of making a public row over it? Indeed, may she not be acting as courteously about Guingamor's garment as he does later about the fairy's? May not Marie have intended this parallelism?" [8] No, we must reply, she may *not* be acting courteously, as there is not a trace of courtesy in her actions at any point. Her motivation in returning the cloak, which seems quite clear in context, is certainly fear for herself. She does not intend a direct accusation of the knight, and does not want to have in her possession any evidence which might call the incident to the attention of anyone, least of all the king. It *is* possible, however, that the lay's anonymous author intended this return-of-clothing episode as a *contrast* —not a parallel— to Guingamor's later return of the fay's garments when the damsel shames him for taking them, [9] a possibility

---

[7] *Op. cit.*, p. 12.
[8] *Op. cit.*, p. 973.
[9] H. Newstead offers an explanation for the behavior of both queen and fairy in terms of role-elaborations. Scholars have attempted to use the varied nature of the fay Morgain's prototype to explain the differing

to be considered in connection with the knight's encounter with the fay.

The third element is that of the blush, for which ingenious explanations have been advanced. In Damon's imaginative conception of the lay, the poem's author has "changed the original brute Graelent into a blushing, courteous youth on the verge of first love," [10] and the queen's return of Guingamor's mantle is to be interpreted as evidence that she is a decent person "terrified at her act." On the basis of his hypothesis concerning the procedure of the poetess, Damon asserts that "Marie certainly had it in her mind to contrast this queen (who is evidently not evil, though dominated by her feelings twice: the first time when on the way to chapel she sees Guingamor, and the second time when after dinner she fears his moodiness will betray her) with the sensual and more experienced queen in *Lanval* (Guenevere, who was notorious as an adulteress, who breaks out into shocking speech at the time of her disappointment, and who then in a fit of rage attempts the Egyptian trick, though without the evidence.)" The contention that the queen is not wicked is apparently based on the fact that she returns to Guingamor the mantle which she had snatched from him, and especially on the fact that "we see her first on her way to chapel; we must pity her that 'ariere s'en vait' (55): for after all, Courtly Love approved such turnings aside." [11] But the relevance of Courtly Love's approval to the present situation is not explained; nor does he consider that this very mention of the queen's turning aside on her way to the chapel

---

personalities of the fay who appears in various romances, and Newstead carries this attempt a step further, using it to explain two different ladies in a single poem. Noting that Morgain assumes the role of a woman scorned in love as well as that of fairy mistress, Newstead says that "although Morgain herself is the heroine of two such apparently incompatible traditions, when the two themes happen to be combined they are usually —but not always— assigned to different persons. Hence in the lais of *Guingamor*, *Graelent*, and *Launfal*, the motif of despised love so frequently attached to Morgain is represented by the amorous queen whose rejected love turns to hate and who plots to destroy the hero, and the counter-motif, also originally connected with Morgain, is represented by the fay who becomes the mistress of the hero and frustrates the queen's evil designs" ("Partonopeus," p. 937).

[10] *Op. cit.*, p. 973.
[11] *Loc. cit.*

may be intended to emphasize, not that she is basically "good," but that the action to which she is led by her desire for the young knight is one which is sharply incompatible with all which the chapel represents. Damon's interpretation of Guingamor's part in the dialogue with the queen also reveals a misconception; when the queen tells him that he should love her, says Damon, "the stupid boy answers that he does, for is she not the king's wife? A third time she speaks, and kisses him; he understands at last, blushes, is speechless, and flees."[12] According to this view, the explanation for every action and every word in the encounter is to be found in the fact that Guingamor is a "blushing boy;" his replies are the result of youth and naiveté at first, and his flight is the result of his surprise; his quick "blush" is occasioned by embarrassment combined with an awakening awareness of love.[13] But such an interpretation overlooks the stress placed by the poet on the fact that Guingamor's reply is considered, and that it is "senez."

The inclusion of these three elements indicates that the poet is not merely utilizing a situation which had in his time become a popular motif.[14] The dialogue between the queen and Guingamor and the inclusion of the mantle episode make it probable that, for whatever reason, the poet is patterning his account closely on the story of Joseph and Potiphar's wife. Joseph's wisdom and modesty are brought out in the medieval elaborations of the temptation scene by a device just such as that used in the lay, as

---

[12] *Ibid.*, p. 987.

[13] The *poet's* version, "grant honte en a, tout en rogi," gives an impression of an emotion rather more serious than the adolescent agitation and embarrassment described by Damon.

[14] The fact that the poet represents the offending woman as a queen does not offer evidence that he was not following the Biblical episode closely. The setting of the royal court was of course traditional for such tales of *aventure*, and in this particular tale especially it is effective in heightening the significant central idea. In addition, as Faverty points out, Potiphar's wife is replaced by a queen even in early Bible translations. Tertullian makes Joseph the slave of Pharoah and the temptress the queen, and "at least four Old French verse translations of the Bible contain it: Herman de Valenciennes, *La Bible des sept estaz du monde* by Geoffrey de Paris, Jehan Malkaraume, and the *Traduction Anonyme de la Bible Entière*" (*op. cit.*, p. 103).

he counters each suggestive remark of Potiphar's wife.[15] As Faverty notes, the *Genesis* account is necessarily brief: "And it came to pass, as she spake to him day by day, that he hearkened not unto her" (xxxix, 10), but "later writers multiply Joseph's temptations, thus making him a nobler character through his resistance."[16] Guingamor appears similarly wise, and the poet chose to underline this wisdom by noting that he replied "comme senez."

The mantle element is an important part of the story of Joseph and Potiphar's wife. In the Christian elaborations of the episode, it in fact developed as a test of the truth of the queen's accusations; when she produces it as evidence that the knight had attempted to violate her, the judgment depends on whether it is torn in front (indicating a struggle and therefore guilt) or in back (indicating innocence).[17]

The third element not found in other romance versions, that of the knight's reddening with shame at the queen's proposals, also points to the Biblical origin. The Biblical Joseph was the servant of God although the slave of Potiphar, and his rejection of Potiphar's wife was not in terms of loyalty to his master Potiphar exclusively, but rather in terms of a higher loyalty; his ideal, which he refuses to betray, is religious and moral. In the early elaborations of the story, when Potiphar's wife speaks to Joseph of the sweetness of love, he replies praising the sweetness of God's service, pure love as contrasted to guilt.[18] Examination of the *Guingamor*-poet's comment when the young knight finds he cannot deflect the queen's guilty declaration reveals that this contrast is relevant to the lay also. Guingamor has replied to the queen's talk of love with the assertion that indeed he should love her, as the wife of his king; but when even this ploy fails and she kisses him,

---

[15] Some examples cited by Faverty (pp. 109-14) include Jewish legends, Mohammedan versions, the *Leyendas de José*, the Middle-English *Genesis and Exodus*, the *Cursor Mundi*, the *Mistére du Viel Testament*, and the free English version *Iacob and Iosep*.

[16] *Op. cit.*, p. 109.

[17] *Ibid.*, p. 117.

[18] This is found, for example, in Jewish legend, the Arabic versions, and the Spanish *Leyendas de José*; see Faverty, pp. 110-11.

> Guingamor entent qu'ele dit
> Et quele amor ele requist:
> Grant honte en a, tout en rogi. (vv. 107-109)

It is the *type* of love which she is demanding which causes his feeling of shame, and the poet is quite explicit about this point. What type of love is it? Sensual attraction, lust, passion forbidden, and Guingamor does not even attempt to reply to such an outburst; he hastens away, but not before she has torn from him his cloak in an effort to detain him.

Faverty points out that "to the Fathers of the Church in the Middle Ages Joseph was the great prefiguration of Christ... Into this comparative scheme Potiphar's wife fitted very neatly: Joseph was tempted by her, Christ by the doctors in the synagogue."[19] This analogue is extended to describe Potiphar's wife herself as "a symbol of the synagogue accustomed to commit adultery with strange gods," an interpretation of which Faverty quotes numerous examples. She is also made to represent other evils in the Christian view. For St. Bruno Astens, for example, she represents idolatry, and his elaboration is of interest: "Sed quid per uxorem Putiphar, nisi idolatriam intelligimus? Cui, quia Joseph et SS. martyres consentire noluerunt, quasi sacrilegi et adulteri, et carceri et morti, et exsilio damnati sunt. Cum hac enim meretrice Israel fornacatus est, de quo dicitur: 'Fornacatus est Israel post deos gentium."[20]

Thus we find that Potiphar's wife in medieval exegesis was frequently allegorized, and always in a very unflattering light as "enim meretrice" or a variant. Such was her notoriety. When the evolving story became connected with a queen instead of with Potiphar's wife, and in lays such as *Lanval* was applied to Guenevere who had something of a reputation of her own, the tone changed accordingly. But we have seen that the *Guingamor*-poet's interest in the episode is apparently somewhat different than that of the authors of *Lanval* and *Graelent*. While utilizing the personage of the queen, as did his contemporaries, he remains much more faithful to the Biblical story itself. Is he perhaps by using

---

[19] *Ibid.*, p. 127.
[20] Quoted in *loc. cit.*

it making a strong statement based on Christian interpretation of that story? If so, his method is not unique in the medieval period, even as applied to this particular incident; in the *Livre du Chevalier de la Tour Landry*, for example, the Joseph story is specifically included as "an ensaumple upon this synne of lechery." [21]

Not an idle episode of Courtly Love, then, but sin, and the very serious charge of lechery; did the *Guingamor*-poet intend to introduce something so serious into his poem? This question must be kept in mind while considering the events to which the introductory episode immediately gives rise.

II. THE CHALLENGE OF THE BOAR-HUNT

The next group of questions are centered on the queen's choice of the boar-hunt as her means of ridding herself of the knight. Segre considers the choice to be weak, even ridiculous: "la maggior drammaticità di Guingamor rimane, per vero, spreccata, se tutta la vendetta della regina consiste nella proposta pubblica di una caccia al *blanc porc*, in cui poi non si afferra bene perché Guingamor debba ritenersi chiamato personalmente in causa." [22] But on the narrative level, the queen's choice of the boar-hunt is at least comprehensible, even dramatic: the hunt is known to be extremely dangerous, and she feels sure that if Guingamor undertakes it she will be rid of him permanently. Unlike Potiphar's wife, she apparently chooses not to accuse the knight to the king, but she must separate him from the court. The device, then, is not inappropriate in terms of this objective. The important question is whether the poet intended for it more than its mere adequate functioning in the narrative. Is there something particularly appropriate about a boar-hunt in this particular case?

Stories of hunts were common, as was the hunt itself. We find this element in very frequent association with fairy-mistress tales, notably in *Guigemar* and in *Graelent*; [23] the hunt for the

---

[21] *Ibid.*, p. 105.
[22] *Op. cit.*, p. 761.
[23] The white stag appears also in Wauchier's *Graal* continuation and in *Tydorel*, with variations in the *Didot Perceval*, the Dutch *Lancelot*, *Peredur*, the *Huth Merlin*, and Malory. See Loomis, *Arthurian Tradition*, pp. 68-69.

white stag, or hind, or doe was a famed custom of Arthurian romance, and we remember in particular the stag-hunt in *Erec*, with the successful hunter entitled to bestow a kiss upon the fairest damsel. Scholars have generally grouped the pursuit of these white animals with pursuit of the boar, as any of these may serve as fairy messengers. In this capacity, Kittredge tells us, "the animal is not an ordinary beast but a magical creature in the service of the *fée*, and may even be a transformed fairy maiden."[24] Kittredge, who considers *Guingamor* to present an example of this type, also provides a very important reminder, that the mysterious animal is not limited to fairy-mistress tales: "one of the chief services which they afford is to guide or convey the hero, and in this capacity they are just as usable in one type of tale as in the other... the presence of such a beast in any folk-tale or romantic poem does not even create a presumption that the heroine is a *fée*, unless we can make sure that the creature acts as her messenger or agent. This once determined, we may safely entrust ourselves to the animal's guidance."[25] It is precisely this role of the animal as the *fée's* messenger or agent which we have found to be lacking in *Guingamor*.

Is there any significance in the *Guingamor*-poet's choice of the boar as the object of the hunt? Segre offers as explanation that "il trovare poi in Guigemar e in Graelent una *bisse blance*, e vice versa in Guingamor, ci svela il tentativo, da parte di Guingamor, di occultare l'imitazione di Graelent."[26] Nothing could be more simple. This interpretation, however, based on the assumption that the author of the lay was concerned only with telling an interesting tale while concealing as nearly as possible his very extensive copying, does not resist careful scrutiny. The mere change of the quarry from a hind to a boar would hardly be enough to disguise the imitation; if the story itself is most important, surely the mere inclusion of the hunt and of its results would betray any such attempt at concealment, regardless of the choice of animal.

---

[24] *Op. cit.*, p. 231.
[25] *Ibid.*, p. 235.
[26] *Op. cit.*, p. 758.

If we compare other instances of hunts which lead to encounters with fays we find a significant contrast to *Guingamor*. In *Graelent* and *Guigemar*, for example, the hero happens upon the enchanted animal which is to be his introduction to the Otherworld in the course of what seems to be a perfectly ordinary hunting expedition in the forest. The fay has made arrangements for the encounter, but of this the hero is totally unaware. In *Guingamor*, however, special significance is attached to the boar from its first mention. The queen's reference to it is full of scorn for the knights who fear to undertake its pursuit:

> 'Molt vos oi,' fet ele, 'vanter,
> Et vos aventures conter.
> Mes n'a ceanz nul si hardi,
> De toz iceus que je voi ci,
> Que en la forest ci defors,
> La ou converse li blans pors,
> Osast chacier ne soner cor,
> Qui le donroit mil livres d'or.
> En merveilleus los le metroit,
> Qui le sengler prendre porroit.' (vv. 153-62)

She is challenging them, then, to an *aventure* of the most dangerous kind. It is not, apparently, considered so dangerous because the boar itself is a dangerous beast, for we know that wild boars were common enough as objects of the hunt. Rather, the fearful element is that those who pursue this boar become lost and never return. As the king replies to the queen,

> Onques nus hom n'i pot aler
> Qui puis em peust reperier,
> Por qoi le porc peust chacier;
> La lande i est aventureuse
> Et la riviére perilleuse.
> Molt grant dommage i ai eu:
> Diz chevaliers i ai perdu,
> Toz les meillors de ceste terre,
> Qui le sengler alérent querre. (vv. 174-82)

None of the knights respond to the queen's implied challenge, but Guingamor knows well that it is intended as a trap for him alone. He goes to the king and announces his determination to undertake this dangerous *aventure*.[27]

Two questions are most important concerning this development, which actually sets the stage for the hero's entrance into the Otherworld. In the first place, why is this challenge of the queen, spoken in the presence of the assembled knights, immediately recognized by Guingamor as a trap?

> Guingamor a bien entendu
> Qu'elle a por lui cest plet meu. (vv. 164-65)

In the second place, why, if he knows it to be a trap, does he accept the challenge? He is, after all, guiltless, and there is no indication that the queen is likely to reproduce the revenge attempt of Potiphar's wife by accusing him. On the contrary, here it is the queen who fears being denounced, and Guingamor has nothing to fear. Yet he immediately responds to this challenge, with such determination that even the king's strong opposition cannot deter him.

Both of these questions suggest that the significance of the pursuit of the boar was perhaps greater than that of a mere dangerous task, a means as convenient as any other for ridding the queen of the knight.[28] We know that medieval thought readily assigned symbolic and allegorical interpretations to every manner of thing, as evidenced for example by the numbers of lapidaries

---

[27] Damon's singular interpretation of the hunt in the poem offers in explanation of the hero's willing undertaking of such a dangerous task that it in fact symbolizes a test of virility; the hunt, he says, is the hunt for love, which became the later *Jagdallegorie*, and the young knight, who felt his virility was called into question by the "blushing" encounter with the queen, was eager to undertake the hunt in order to demonstrate that he was not, after all, the failure which he might seem. His eagerness to return to the court to relate his *aventure* would be based, then, on his conquest of the fay, about which he wishes to boast.

[28] W. P. Ker, who shares Damon's opinion that the queen is not entirely bad, sees this choice as a demonstration of the better side of her nature: "being less cruel than other queens of similar fortune, she planned nothing worse than to send him into the *lande aventureuse*, a mysterious forest on the other side of the river, to hunt the wild boar" (*Epic and Romance*, London, 1908, p. 388). Such a view ignores the significance and danger which the poet is careful to emphasize.

and bestiaries in the period. R. T. Holbrook has said that "never was there a time when creatures not men had so wide and curious a hold on the fancy of moralisers and of those who carried out their commands. If we would appreciate that age we must somehow contrive to cast off for a while our deeper knowledge of the animal world... we must cease to believe ourselves the common sharers of natural law, imagining once more that the world was created for us alone; yet, in that very exclusion we must regard our fellows in the animal kingdom as having a spiritual significance. They must become tokens of the vices or virtues of this world and of the world to come." [29] With this in mind, we may seek a clue to the significance of the boar-hunt in medieval animal symbolism. Does the boar commonly represent something more than a traditional object of the hunt?

In his study of myth and allegory Pépin cites an early example of the tendency to associate animals symbolically with moral characteristics of either a positive or a negative type. The author of the pseudo-*Epître de Barnabé*, in the first half of the second century, allegorized the ritual prescriptions of the Old Testament in terms of a prefiguration of the Messiah. "Les animaux dont la consommation est proscrite (*Lévit*. XI; *Deut*. XIV, 3-21) expriment symboliquement l'interdiction notifiée à tout chrétien de ressembler par son caractère à ces animaux, ou même de fréquenter qui leur ressemble." [30] Druce, discussing various metaphorical uses of swine, lists a number of appearances in the Gospel:

> Again, pigs are the unclean and wanton men in the Gospel: "If thou cast us out, send us into the herd of swine." Again in the same: "Cast not thy pearles before swine." Swine are the unclean spiritis in the gospel. "And he sent him into his fields to feed swine." The pig also similarly signifies the unclean men and sinners about whom it is written in the psalm, "With thy hid treasure is their belly filled — they are filled with swine's flesh and have left what they have over to their little ones." For this speaks of uncleannesses which are hidden from God, that is, which are known to be forbidden. Swine's

---

[29] *Dante and the Animal Kingdom* (New York, 1966), 10.
[30] J. Pépin, *Mythe et Allégorie* (Paris, 1958), 263.

flesh belongs to polluted things, which, among other precepts of the old testament, are prescribed as unclean.[31]

In discussing the symbolism developed by Christianity to reach the masses and to express metaphysical ideas difficult to represent in other ways, Maury has this to say of the pig: "Le porc, animal impur, frappé de réprobation par les Juifs et les Egyptiens; le porc, dans le corps duquel l'Evangile nous montre le démon allant chercher un refuge au sortir du corps du possédé, devait naturellement devenir un symbole du diable. Il fut particulièrement destiné à représenter le démon de la gourmandise, de la volupté des plaisirs immondes; de là, la croyance populaire que l'esprit tentateur grogne comme un porc et se montre sous cette forme dans ses effrayantes apparitions. Le porc, placé aux pieds d'un saint, signifie donc le démon et les voluptés vaincues, asservies."[32] Maury quotes in this regard from R. P. Th. Taynaud:

> Et vitam quidem voluptuariam porcorum esse D. Chrysostomus diserte tradit: Necnon S. Nilus in opere de octo vitiis, cum de gula: Obesus belluo, inquit, porcus est ad caedam paratus. Praeiverantque Novatianus et Clement Alexandrinus atque Lactantius, inquirentes quorsum Deus suem Judaeis edulem esse prohiberet: 'Cum lex, inquit Novatianus, suem cibo prohibet assumi, reprehendit suum non in animi generositate, sed in sola carne ponentem.' Clemens vero in eamdem sententiam disserens ait idcirco vetitum fuisse porco vesci: 'Nam porcus, quod est animal voluptati deditum et immundum, ciborum cupiditatem et salacem in se venerea libidinem adinquinatam significat intemperantiam, materialemque et in luteo jacentem et quae ad caedem pinquescit et interitum.'[33]

J.-B. Casalii presents the same symbolic interpretation for the conquered boar ("Sus ab pedes sancti Antonii denotat sensuales voluptates quas ille conculcaverat").[34]

---

[31] G. C. Druce, "The Sow and Pigs: A Study in Metaphor," *Archaeologia Cantiana,* xlvi, 5-6.
[32] *Op. cit.,* pp. 254-55.
[33] Quoted in Maury, p. 255, from the *Symbolicas S. Antonii magni imagines Commentarius.*
[34] Quoted in *loc. cit.,* from the *De Veteribus Sacris Christianorum ritibus.*

This Christian-moral symbolism of swine has, as Pépin notes, its pagan homologue in "l'interprétation cynico-stoicienne de l'épisode de Circe," [35] and the examples of allegorical interpretation of Scripture find their place within a wider framework of presentations of swine as emblems of moral degradation. Boethius states that if a man "is immersed in foul and filthy lusts, he is kept down in a swine's slough." [36] Vincent de Beauvais (*Speculum morale*, lib. III, dis. III, pars IX, col. 1383) says that "Luxuriosi sunt sicut sus, qui libertius habet nares in stercoribus quam in floribus." Holbrook, who notes the preceding example, devotes a chapter to Dante's use of swine, pointing out that for him they are the "abomination." In Purgatory XIV the people of Casentino are likened to swine, and "Benvenuto da Imola, whose capacity as a historian is notable, affirms that these swine are the Counts Guido, whom Dante rightly calls swine, for their foul lust. Once these counts held sway over the city of Ravenna, but in the people's rage were almost all slaughtered on account of their uncurbed lechery." Boccaccio makes the same connection: "La lussuria per la sua brutezza è somigliata al porco." [37] From a variety of sources of different periods, George Ferguson says that the hog represents "the demon of sensuality and gluttony," [38] and J. E. Cirlot, that it may stand for licentiousness. [39]

We must next inquire whether this symbolism is relevant to the puzzling question of why the queen proposed the particular challenge of the boar-hunt to Guingamor, why he recognized it as such, and why he accepted it at once. What do we know of the boar in this poem? We know what the king and the queen tell us: that it has never been hunted successfully, that the "best" knights of the court —ten of them— have gone off in its pursuit and have not returned, and that for this reason this *aventure* is regarded with particular dread.

---

[35] *Op. cit.*, p. 263.
[36] *The Consolation of Philosophy*, IV, Pr. III; trsl. James J. Buchanan (New York, 1957), 43.
[37] Holbrook, pp. 170-71.
[38] *Signs and Symbols in Christian Art* (New York, 1961), 20.
[39] *A Dictionary of Symbols*, trsl. from the Spanish by Jack Sage (New York, 1962), 29.

Hofer is of the opinion that in connecting the episodes of attempted seduction and boar-hunt the poet simply forgot the thread of his narrative.[40] Other scholars too have considered the introductory episode irrelevant to the main part of the poem, citing it as an example of the poet's ineptitude. Schofield accounts for this supposed lapse in a poem which he finds otherwise well-handled by terming it a late addition: "It is evident that this story of the depravity of the wife in high station was originally extraneous to our account."[41] Hoepffner is equally severe: "Pour amener la chasse du porc blanc, l'auteur n'a rien trouvé de mieux qu'une scène de séduction analogue à celle de *Lanval*. Le morceau, à vrai dire, n'a aucun rapport avec l'aventure principale."[42] But if the poem follows the Potiphar's-wife story more closely than contemporary versions of the same motif because the poet intended to signal a transgression on the part of the queen which was not courtly but of a more serious nature, the choice of the boar appears highly significant.[43] As Faverty said of the queen's role in partial analogues of the Potiphar's-wife story, "the revenge she takes may differ in each case according to the ingenuity of the

---

[40] "Recht ungeschickt ist die Begründing in Guingamor, denn hier fürchtet die Königen, der Ritter, dem nach dieser Vorfall selbst nicht wohl zu Mute ist, werde ihr Verhalten seinem Onkel mitteilen. Dabei vergisst der Dichter, dass ihn für diesen Fall das Potiphar-motif ja schon ein weitere Lösung, die Anklage der Königen wie in *Lanval*, in die Hand gab. Allerdings hätte er dann den Mantel nicht an Guingamor zuruckstellen dürfen" (*op. cit.*, p. 367).
[41] "Guingamor," p. 237.
[42] "Lais anonymes," pp. 10-11.
[43] William S. Woods points out that in the general plot formula common to four of Chrétien's romances, there is a point at which the hero is "made aware of some error or fault or of some less obvious reason which forces him to abandon his lofty pinnacle of happiness." Such awareness is that which is forced upon Guingamor. As Woods rightly notes, "this point in the plot can be likened to the initial impulse of a drama for it serves to motivate the main body of the poem which is a series of adventures concerned with the hero's efforts to recover his former status, presumably through his becoming more deserving of it by the correction of his error or by the expiation of this fault" ("The Plot Structure in Four Romances of Chrétien de Troyes," *Studies in Philology*, L, 1953, p. 4). In *Guingamor* the hero is seeking through his *aventure* not to recover his former status, as the fault-impetus is not in him, but to prove his moral strength, and thus in a sense to overcome that which has been revealed to him as a weakness in his society.

author," [44] and it seems probable that here the author is exercising his ingenuity to combine two types of tales both of which are readily adaptible to his own intent.

It is obvious that the queen's tone in addressing the assembled members of Arthur's court is one of mockery. If we consider the boar as a symbol of licentiousness, the challenge is heavy with sarcasm; no one else has been able to conquer the boar; should not a young knight who prides himself on his virtue to the extent of resisting the advances even of his queen have a try? The king and all the knights, with the single exception of Guingamor, do not dare to undertake this particular *aventure*. Guingamor, on the contrary, accepts the challenge quickly. Such a situation is not uncommon in medieval romance; in many Round Table episodes only one knight is qualified to accept and to accomplish a particular quest, with all others doomed to failure. In this instance, Guingamor recognizes the queen's challenge as a trap for him because only he among the knights is aware of what has happened during the absence of the king and his retinue, thus only he can fully appreciate the mockery and scorn of her mention of the boar, and its implications. The queen's challenge is, in other words, a moral one. The young knight, feeling sure of his virtue, is confident of success, and this confidence explains also why he is "liez" after obtaining the king's permission to undertake the *aventure*. The animal is not dangerous for what it is in itself, but for what it represents, and this Guingamor feels he need not fear. Thus the queen's choice of the pursuit of the boar is completely appropriate, and the Potiphar's-wife episode is clearly a necessary part of this induction to the hero's Otherworld visit, not an extraneous element.

Interpretations based on animal symbolism have been seriously advanced for various medieval works, as for example for *Gawain and the Green Knight*, in which its function is no more obvious on the superficial level than in the present lay. Savage and other scholars have suggested that each of the hunting scenes in that work parallels another, essentially moral, scene taking place between Gawain and the wife of his host, and that the key to the

---

[44] *Op. cit.*, p. 80.

significance of these encounters is found in the nature of the animals hunted on each day.[45] More recently, Nitze has discussed the lion in *Yvain* as a symbolic element. Noting that the lion, with its watchfulness, is commonly considered a symbol of Christ, he asserts that the association of the lion with the chastized knight, who had been hitherto governed by pride, indicates the piety which now guides Yvain's actions.[46] Other examples of this type may be readily found.

Thus Guingamor, to the dismay of all except himself, sets out to hunt the wild boar. As noted previously, scholars have generally seen this boar-hunt in *Guingamor* as a parallel to the hunts in which other knights encounter enchanted animals and are led to a waiting fairy mistress, and have thus considered the pursuit of the boar a typical fairy-mistress induction. However, in the fairy-messenger animal appearances, the hunter seems to happen upon the animal during the course of an ordinary hunt in the forest, while in *Guingamor* the hunt itself is a well-known *aventure* which the hero undertakes in a very deliberate way. No fairy-messenger concept is needed to explain why he pursues the boar, and if the interpretation proposed for the first section of the lay is correct, the hero's pursuit of the boar is far more than a mere narrative device to lead him to the fay. It is rather a very significant trial of his moral fortitude. The fact of pursuit is in itself significant. Bezzola notes that "la chasse avait au moyen âge, dès l'époque carolingienne, une valeur symbolique... elle était pour l'Eglise le symbole de la conversion du pécheur ou de la chasse à la vertu."[47] The final decision as to whether the boar is fairy-related, however, must be based on what happens when Guingamor finally encounters the fay.

---

[45] *Op. cit.*, pp. 5-6.
[46] W. A. Nitze, "Yvain and the Myth of the Fountain," *Speculum*, XXX (1955), 170-79.
[47] R. R. Bezzola, *Le Sens de l'Aventure et de l'Amour* (Paris, 1947), 258, n. 34. Bezzola considers that in the *Erec* this tendency to consider the hunt symbolically remains, but that in that work and in "l'art profane" generally, it has become "la chasse à la joie que procurait l'amour de la beauté. La chasse devenait ainsi pour le poète courtois un symbole de la vie humaine comme le voyait le chevalier."

III. An Unusual Fairy Mistress for an Unusual Otherworld Guest

Guingamor follows the boar through the forest and over the *lande*, and across the river which traditionally divides Faërie from the mortal world. He finds the fay bathing, and takes her clothes, but does not intend to stay; rather, his plan is to continue his pursuit of the boar, and to return to the damsel when his hunt has been successful. The incidents of his encounter with the fay and of his stay in the Otherworld give rise to our third group of related questions: why does he not forget his hunt when he encounters the fay? Why does she address him in a rather atypical manner? Why does he at first refuse her invitation? Why does she tell him that he can have the boar only with her aid? And finally, what are we to assume about the nature of this Otherworld?

Guingamor in finding the fay bathing and in taking her clothes has counterparts in other knights who enter the Otherworld, but unlike them, he does not intend to remain. The fay calls to him to leave her clothes, and as we have seen, both the tone of this appeal and its content are unusual in tales of this type. Her tactic is to shame him:

> Guingamors, lessiez ma despoille.
> Ja Deu ne place ne ne voille
> Qu'entre chevaliers soit retret
> Que vos faciez si grant mesfet
> D'embler les dras d'une meschine
> En l'espoisse de la gaudine. (vv. 447-52)

Why does she choose this particular approach? It may be because she knows that it is likely to succeed; and it is likely to succeed because she is accusing him of doing a thing which is inconsistent with his hero-role. Taking the clothes of a damsel is an act of which he must not, especially while engaged on his present *aventure*, be guilty, and it is possible that her mention of God as the being whose opinion is important in this matter is more than conventional. Guingamor reacts immediately; he goes to her and gives her the clothing. It is quite possible that the poet here presents a contrast (not a parallel, as Damon would have it) to the action of the queen, who gives up Guingamor's mantle not from shame but from fear. If the queen's action is lustful and guilty, Guingamor's action here is the resisting of the temptation to similar tendencies.

The fay does more than reproach the hero: she invites him to remain with her. But Guingamor will not be turned from his purpose, and refuses because he has lost the boar and the brachet, which he must continue to pursue. Is he, as Damon suggests, in this a "stupid boy?" Or is this modification of the typical fairy-mistress pattern further evidence that the poet has something different in mind than merely a good story? If the pursuit of the boar in this lay may be interpreted as a test of the young knight's virtue, a test to which the queen's actions and her mocking words have set him, it is not surprising that the sight of a fay is not enough to turn him completely aside. He is momentarily distracted, momentarily tempted, and yields to this impulse to the extent of seizing the damsel's clothing; yet when she reproaches him with his action, he at once recognizes that the reproach is just, and returns the garments. He then refuses her invitation because he must complete his perilous task.

Although scholars have not understood the attitude on the part of Guingamor which prompts his return of the maiden's clothing and his initial refusal of her invitation, the fairy herself seems to understand it perfectly well. She explains to him that only with her aid can he have the boar; she promises it to him, and on these terms only —"par tel covent"— is he willing to remain with her.

It is now necessary to attempt to answer another, and perhaps more difficult, question. Is this involvement of a fairy completely inappropriate if, as here contended, the lay is fundamentally the story of the testing of a young knight's particular moral qualities? In Moorman's opinion the code of knightly conduct in relation to love is fundamental in the romances of Chrétien, which "say that love properly conceived and followed is the basis of chivalric virtue and true knighthood and, contrariwise, that love falsely conceived and followed is the destruction of knightly society;"[48] in *Guingamor* it is likely that "love falsely conceived and followed" is contrasted to "love properly conceived and followed" in a very deliberate way in Guingamor's encounters with the queen and with the fairy. Nonetheless, if this fay is the typical fairy mistress of lay and romance, who draws the hero to her for her own delight and keeps him under her spell in the Otherworld, the answer is clearly that her presence here *is* inappropriate, and that the poet perhaps intended only a pleasant fairy-mistress adventure after all. But is she the typical fairy mistress?

As already seen, the typical fairy-mistress framework does not suffice to explain a number of elements in the poem. This fay apparently has not sent the boar as a messenger to the knight; she apparently has not been in command of his actions; she does not command now, as Schofield tells us that a true fay must,[49] but rather persuades him by means of a reproach which he recognizes as well-founded. There is no evidence of a fairy "retention." In fact, consideration of the Otherworld-voyage type of tale led us to the conclusion that this voyage of Guingamor to the Otherworld, which is so prominent in the lay, seems closer to the early Celtic Otherworld conception than to the later adventures of knights who are led, or who stray, into Faërie. The appearance is that of Faërie, certainly, as are most of the descriptive terms, but the induction and the atmosphere are more like those experienced by Bran, who, like Guingamor, was specially qualified to undertake a voyage to the Otherworld. The *Guingamor* fay is part of an Otherworld which is not a momentary manifestation of Faërie, like the *Val sans Retor* or the *Chastel Orgueilleus*. She did not create this Otherworld, nor does she control it, although she apparently has some control over the boar which she promises to Guingamor and in fact gives to him at the end of his stay with her. She does not command in this Otherworld, although she may persuade. But if she does not command, and if she is not responsible for Guingamor's voyage to the Otherworld, why, for purposes of the poem, is she there at all?

---

[48] C. Moorman, *A Knyght There Was: The Evolution of the Knight in Literature* (Lexington, 1967), 54.
[49] "Guingamor," p. 236.

A clue to her presence may be found in the Christianization of certain elements of fairy myth and legend. Although fairies were frequently assigned to the realm of demons and considered practitioners of black magic, they were often credited with the practice of white magic, a conception utilized by many medieval writers. We have seen that in works such as *Yonec* and *Partonopeus de Blois*, the supernatural personage demonstrates a belief in Christianity before becoming the *ami* or *amie* of a mortal. Fairies are occasionally mistaken for the Virgin. In *Yvain*, as Nitze points out, "the very help he [the hero] gets is God-given —so that Morgain the Fay (*la sage*) who provides the magic salve for the healing of his mind is dependent in 2948 on the help of God (*a l'aïe de De*) for its effect."[50]

Cirlot in his fundamental study of symbolism explains the use of animals and fairies in terms which are relevant to the present discussion. According to Jung, he reports, "the animal stands for the non-human psyche, for the world of sub-human instincts, and for the unconscious areas of the psyche. The more primitive the animal, the deeper the stratum of which it is an expression."[51] He states also that "in the struggle between a knight and a wild or fabulous animal —one of the most frequent themes in symbolism— the knight's victory can consist either in the death or in the taming of the animal."[52] Guingamor at the lay's end considers his hunt successful despite the fact that he does not actually kill the boar himself; thus the object of his *aventure* must be the destruction of the boar, victory over it simply. The help of the fay in achieving that victory does not lessen its significance.

What then is the fairy's role? To Cirlot, "fairies probably symbolize the supra-normal powers of the human soul, at least in the forms in which they appear in esoteric works. Their nature is contradictory: they fulfill humble tasks, yet possess extraordinary powers. They bestow gifts upon the newly born; they can cause people, palaces and wonderful things to appear out of thin air; they dispense riches (as a symbol of wisdom). Their powers, however, are not simply magical, but are rather the

---

[50] *Op. cit.*, p. 117.
[51] *Op. cit.*, p. 13.
[52] *Ibid.*, p. 9.

sudden revelation of latent possibilities... Fairies are, in short, personifications of stages in the development of the spiritual life or in the 'soul' of landscapes." [53] We have seen that fairies are "generally regarded as of a nature between spirits and men... a separate race of superior beings," [54] which is entirely consistent with their symbolic use as representative of "supra-normal powers of the soul." Even Lucy Paton says in discussing the fays of Arthurian romance that the usual character or tradition of the hero "frequently transforms the part of the fay from its original state." [55] If the boar represents lechery, a baser instinct in man, and Guingamor's hero-role is to defeat it, it is plausible that the fay with her "superior" qualities should be able to help the knight to overcome the boar. The nature of her address to him when he takes her clothes is in this light entirely appropriate.

It may be objected that a fairy-mistress theme, by its very nature, is an unlikely element in a quest whose purpose is the overcoming of something such as lechery, and certainly the fairy mistresses of Lanval and Graelent, for all their contrast to the guilty and vengeful queen, seem unlikely candidates for the role of assistants in such an undertaking. They offer *druerie,* and while their relation to the hero is elevated by an element of chivalrous refinement, it is hardly a Christian conception, but rather one of Faërie existing on its own terms. In *Guingamor* too the fay becomes the *amie* of the knight; but the situation is clearly not the same.

It is significant that the Otherworld in the lay seems more closely to resemble the Celtic conception than that of Faërie pure and simple. As noted, the fay has apparently not drawn Guingamor to the Otherworld for her own enjoyment. She is not responsible for the Otherworld as it is found in the work; she moves about in it as does the hero, although she has powers which surpass his mortal capabilities, and can thus aid him. The relation of damsel to hero is also important in the Celtic Otherworld-voyage tales; MacCulloch reports that love-making has a significant part in Elysian tales, and that although later redactors of

---

[53] *Ibid.,* p. 96.
[54] MacCulloch, "Fairy," p. 679.
[55] *Op. cit.,* p. 248.

the tales considered the divine visitant who attempts to entice the hero to visit the Otherworld a demon, "on the other hand, the lovemaking which goes on among the peoples of Elysium, even in documents edited by Christian scribes, is said to be 'without sin, without crime' (*Bran* 41)." [56] We have seen that in some early Celtic Otherworld tales the Christian element is prominent, and that the tendency to recognize elements common to both the Celtic Otherworld and the Christian Paradise conceptions led eventually to the identification, in the *imrama*, of Elysium with Paradise or Heaven. [57] The sensuous delights of the Celtic Elysium which became typical of Faërie are not presented with the same tone as those in the strictly fairy-mistress tales. "Sensuous as are many of these characteristics, they yet have a spiritual aspect which must not be overlooked. Thus the emphasis placed on the beauty of the land, its music, its rest, its peace, its oblivion, is more spiritual than sensual, while the dwelling of favored mortals there with divine beings is suggestive of that union with the divine which is the essence of all religions." [58]

The supernatural passage of time in the Otherworld as experienced by Guingamor is easily understood in terms of this pattern. It is another example of the presence of an Otherworld concept which is not that of Faërie, as there is no evidence that it is due to the fay's efforts to keep the hero there. In the early Celtic mentions of the supernatural passage of time in the Otherworld the phenomenon is apparently due to the nature of the Otherworld itself, rather than to a specific enchantment, and it is presented as a strongly positive element, connected with the absence of aging. Furthermore, a major characteristic of the Christian conception of Paradise is the absence of time, thus the absence of aging, affording immortality to the inhabitants. We need not eliminate the possibility of a conception in which both aspects figure simply because we find sensuous delights also described. [59] As Maury

---

[56] "Abode of the Blest," p. 693.
[57] *Ibid.*, p. 695.
[58] *Ibid.*, p. 694.
[59] Maud Bodkin, in *Archetypal Patterns in Poetry: Psychological Studies of Imagination* (London, 1963), presents an interesting psychological interpretation of one main factor predominant in simple forms of the Paradise image: "The blossoming, sunlit garden, the blessed spot, green and

points out concerning the medieval conception of Paradise itself, "le monde terrestre était reproduit tout entier dans le monde invisible, où doit se passer la vie future. Tout y était conçu par le vulgaire sur le modèle des choses d'ici-bas, depuis ces riches costumes dont l'artiste revêtait les personnages divins, et sous lesquels les personnes divines apparaissaient aux imaginations en extase, jusqu'à ce paradis représenté soit comme un véritable lieu de plaisance, étincillant et splendide, soit comme une cité fortifiée..." [60] The inhabitants of the Otherworld, like those of the Christian Paradise, enjoy the absence of sin, as well as that of death, and the Otherworld as described to Bran is obviously influenced by the Christian conception of the state of man before the Fall. Is Guingamor enjoying, during his time spent with the fay, a similar state of innocence?

---

fountainous, which rises before the inward eye of poet and traveller alike, in times of weariness and hardship, appears very simply related to the needs of our nature. We may envisage it in accordance with the law formulated by Freud as the pleasure-principle, which asserts that 'any given process originates in an unpleasant state of tension and thereupon determines for itself such a path that its ultimate issue coincides with a relaxation of this tension.' Amid various circumstances of painful tension, the image of a Paradise of calm and soft luxuriance, 'where life is easiest for man,' fulfils the requirement of this pleasure-principle..." (p. 137).

[60] *Op. cit.*, pp. 176-77. Guingamor's stay in the Otherworld is in the mysterious *palès* which suddenly appears before him and which we later learn is that of his new *amie*. Cirlot's comments on the symbolism of the castle are of the greatest interest here for their suggestion of the possible significance of such enchantments in the fairy material. He notes that it is obviously significant as a Mansion of the Beyond, or as an Entrance to the Other World, and the 'Castle of Light' presents a "redemption" aspect of this image. "Piobb explains that the sudden appearance of a castle in the path of the wanderer is like the sudden appearance of a spiritual pattern. 'Before this fascinating vision, all fatigue disappears. One has the clear impression that treasure lies within. The splendid temple is the achieving of the inconceivable, the materialization of the unexpected.' The castle, in sum, together with the treasure (that is, the eternal essence of spiritual wealth), the damsel (that is, the anima in the Jungian sense) and the purified knight, make up a synthesis expressive of the will to salvation" (pp. 37-38).

IV. Completion of the Cycle

The last group of questions, those concerning Guingamor's departure from the Otherworld and the lay's conclusion, may be used to put the proposed interpretation to the test. It has been noted that one of the ways in which Guingamor's fairy mistress appears atypical is in the nature of the warning which she gives him as he prepares to leave her. This warning, not to eat or drink in the world of mortals, is far from the injunction to secrecy imposed on Lanval and on Graelent. It has nothing to do with her personal relation to the knight, but is rather a warning about a fundamental relation which obtains between the Otherworld and the world of mortals. Guingamor, who cannot believe her when she explains that three hundred years have passed since he came to her and that the court of old is all but forgotten, faces a danger of which only she is aware, and to which she wishes to alert him. At his insistence, he is given his uncle's brachet and the boar's head, as he had been promised, and crosses the river out of the Otherworld while she commends him to God.

This crossing of the river or other barrier, an element prominent in many Otherworld-voyage tales, is the procedure described by Campbell as the crossing of the return threshold, and is highly relevant to the interpretation of the lay. Relating the Otherworld visit of a hero to a deep mythical conception, Campbell points out that

> the equating of a single year in Paradise to one hundred of earthly existence is a motif well known to myth. The full round of one hundred signifies totality... From the standpoint of the Olympians, eon after eon of earthly history rolls by, revealing ever the harmonious form of the total round, so that where men see only change and death, the blessed behold immutable form, world without end. But now the problem is to maintain this cosmic standpoint in the face of an immediate earthly pain or joy. The taste of the fruits of temporal knowledge draws the concentration of the spirit away from the center of the eon to the peripheral crisis of the moment. The

balance of perfection is lost, the spirit falters, and the hero falls. [61]

After crossing the river which is his return threshold, Guingamor learns that the words of the fay were indeed true. He presents the boar's head, token of his conquest, to a *charboniers* whom he urges to relay the story of the *aventure*, and turns to make his way back to the Otherworld. But he is under the influence of the world of mortals now; feeling great hunger, he eats three wild apples from a tree which happens to be in his path, and immediately the privileges of his Otherworld existence vanish. Before the eyes of the astonished *charboniers*, he ages rapidly, so rapidly that the onlooker

> Ne cuidoit mie au sien espoir
> Qu'il peust vivre jusqu'au soir. (vv. 653-54)

As previously noted, this apple episode has been one of the major sources of puzzlement concerning the poem. The basic cause of this puzzlement is that *Guingamor* has been considered in terms of its representation of the fairy-mistress tradition; when confronted by a situation in which the hero eats and becomes subject to the conditions of the land in which he eats, a common motif in fairy lore, scholars have expected to find a parallel to the situation as it commonly appears in tales of fairy enchantment. In the typical fairy spell, the hero partakes of fairy food, or comes in contact in some way with an enchanted substance, and as a result is subject to the full magic effect. The *Guingamor*-poet, the scholars decide, has again demonstrated his ineptitude in his mishandling of this motif. Philipot insisted that the account at one time included the original eating of food in the Otherworld; [62] Schofield concluded that the poet probably simply misplaced the episode. [63]

---

[61] Joseph Campbell, *The Hero with a Thousand Faces* (Cleveland and New York, 1966), 223-24. Cirlot's comment on the ford is also relevant to this conception; it is "an aspect of threshold symbolism, denoting the dividing-line between two states or two forms of reality..." (*op. cit.*, p. 107).

[62] *Op. cit.*, p. 274.

[63] "Guingamor," p. 224.

The failure to take into account the possibility of a symbolic significance for the poem is failure to see the obvious. The apple-eating episode as presented is indeed a strange element in a fairy-mistress tale. If we eliminate for a moment the assumption that it is intended to function in terms of the fairy-mistress type, however, the significance of this eating of fruit in the land of mortals, followed immediately by a fall from a privileged state, appears clearly Christian. The idea of the forbidden fruit, and especially of the apple, is hardly obscure in Christian symbology. Philipot, who insists that *Guingamor* presents an inversion of the usual case in fairy story, himself points out as an example of the overall theme the temptation in the Garden of Eden: " 'Goûtez de cette pomme, dit le serpent de la Génèse, et vous deviendrez semblable à Dieu même';"[64] but he does not recognize the possible significance for *Guingamor* of the Christian representation of the motif. We may be quite certain that the story of the Fall of man connected with eating of the forbidden fruit was as familiar to the medieval poet as the fairy-related versions of the motif.

If, then, the apple-eating incident in *Guingamor* reflects the original incident as a result of which man was expelled from the Earthly Paradise, the significance of the apple in that Biblical episode is relevant. Whatever the specific interpretation attached to it, there can be little doubt that it is connected with an indulgence of man's lower as opposed to his spiritual nature. Cirlot states that the apple "is symbolic of earthly desires, or of the indulgence of such desires. The warning not to eat the forbidden apple came, therefore, from the mouth of the supreme being, as a warning against the exaltation of materialistic desire."[65] T. Inman asserts even that "it is tolerably clear, from all the tales and pictures in which a fruit like the apple figures, that the emblem symbolized a desire for an intimate union between the sexes."[66] Charity and cupidity as the two poles of the medieval scale of values are emphasized by D. W. Robertson, Jr., who notes that

---

[64] *Op. cit.*, p. 272.
[65] *Op. cit.*, p. 14.
[66] *Ancient Pagan and Modern Christian Symbolism* (New York, 1875), 56.

"the fact that the word love (*amor*) could be used for either charity or cupidity opened enormous possibilities for literary word-play." [67] Robertson points out that one often sees *caritas* and *luxuria* opposed rather than *caritas* and *cupiditas*. "When *luxuria* or *fornicatio* is used symbolically, either one well describes the sin of Adam and Eve and may be justly placed as the crowning fruit of the tree of Babylon. The evil tree thus suggests idolatrous sexual love, an extreme form of cupidity and a reflection of the Fall." [68] It is *luxuria* which the queen introduces in the poem and which the boar may represent, and it is thus *luxuria* which is the cause of the quest of Guingamor. Is it not more than coincidence that his return from the Otherworld, his falling back into his fallible and guilt-prone mortal state, is connected with eating an apple, the same act which Christian tradition connects with the Fall? Thus in contrast to the hero of the typical fairy-mistress tale, who suffers because he has broken a commandment of his *amie* and is punished by her for his misdeed, Guingamor suffers because he has failed to heed the fay's warning about the nature of the mortal world to which he returns. He has proven his virtue, and as a reward has been allowed to take back to the mortal world the boar's head, symbol of his victory. But he is still a mortal, and not perfect, and the fay no doubt was aware of this in commending him to God when he took his leave of her. In the world of mortals he acts again like a mortal, and when he feels hunger he eats of mortal food, thus symbolically paralleling the fall of man who in the Garden of Eden betrays spiritual nature to eat of the forbidden fruit. Bodkin's description of the archetypal hero-figure is of one "poised between height and depth, between the Divine and the Devilish, swung forward and upward in reflection of imagination's universal range, hurled back and downward in expression of individual limitation and restraining censure

---

[67] "The Doctrine of Charity in Medieval Literary Gardens," *Speculum*, XXVI (1951), 28.

[68] *Loc. cit.* Maud Bodkin in her discussion of the image of woman notes Milton's use of the Fall story: "Depicting Satan in presence of the tender love-making of Paradise, Milton has already shown him, and the Hell from which he comes, as symbols of destroying lust and envy... The primal sin is felt by Milton to be unbridled passion..." (*op. cit.*, p. 168).

of the whole upon the part."[69] Here the mortal state reasserts itself.

On this point scholars have again failed to detect the relevance of the incident because of their refusal to consider the poem on its own terms. For example, Segre insists that when the poem diverges to any great extent from *Lanval* and *Graelent* "l'azione del *lai* si fa confusa e inconcludente."[70] As an example of this he asserts "che poi il fallo dell'eroe contro l'amata, e la molla della conclusione fiabesca consistano in un peccato di gola (con abondanti particolari sull'appetito di Guingamor) è procedimento, a dir poco, ingenuo."[71] His recognition of the fall of Guingamor as occasioned by a "peccato di gola" did not lead to a consideration of the possible significance of such an episode for the rest of the lay.

Punishment inevitably follows the transgression, but in this case it is not inflicted by the fay; instead, her attendants come for the offender at once, and while rebuking him, carry him gently away. We may suppose that he is being carried back to the Otherworld, as they take him across the river; but what of his fate? Of this we cannot be certain. We have seen that the Otherworld as presented in this poem has its own laws, which are no more in the complete control of the fay than are the mortal world and its laws. Guingamor has transgressed against something more fundamental than the will of his *amie*. It is this uncertainty as to the fate of the hero which adds the strange poignancy to the poem's conclusion.

This carrying away of the enfeebled hero by two mysterious damsels is strongly reminiscent of the famed departure of Arthur from the world of mortals. The partial parallel introduces a further question, that of the hero monomyth. Faral notes Arthur's "aspect de héros national et en quelque sorte messianique,"[72] and there is little doubt that such monomyth is operative in the case

---

[69] *Op. cit.*, p. 245.
[70] *Op. cit.*, p. 762.
[71] *Loc. cit.*
[72] *Légende Arthurienne*, I, p. 244. E. Anwyl in the *Encyclopaedia of Religion and Ethics*, II, 1-7 discusses the tendency to make the king into a Christian hero.

of the king. Of the twenty-two elements which Raglan found to form the pattern of the mythic hero, Arthur's story presents nineteen.[73] We find more than one hint of Arthur's career in *Guingamor*, among the most significant being that of the pursuit of the wild boar, a pursuit which is attributed in legend also to the king. The tale of Arthur's boar hunt is found as early as Nennius, who relates that the king's hound Cabal left a giant footprint in the course of that pursuit, and a boar-hunt in which the king took part is described in detail in *Kulhwch and Olwen*.[74] The boar was called the Twrch Trwyth, and was "in Brythonic legend a knight whose sins caused him to be transformed into a wild boar."[75] Because it caused so much devastation, its capture was one of the tasks imposed on Kulhwch as part of his effort to win the hand of Olwen, and in the hunt Arthur aided the young hero. One may suspect that some of the hero-fame of Arthur is being consciously applied by association to Guingamor.

The elements of the hero-monomyth type actually apparent in *Guingamor* are those which are most central to the conception. The cycle of the hero as Campbell describes it includes a call to adventure, the crossing of a threshold, supernatural aid, temptation, success in the quest undertaken, and a return to the world from which the hero came. It is at once clear that *Guingamor* fits this basic pattern. The hero is challenged, to a highly significant undertaking; he accepts the challenge, crosses the threshold into the Otherworld, is tempted, receives supernatural aid (from the fay), lives a life of joy which rewards his virtue and denotes success in the quest, and finally returns to the mortal world, thinking to return to his uncle's court. Campbell's comments distinguishing the hero type of the typical fairy tale from the composite hero of the monomyth are of the greatest relevance here. The composite monomyth-hero, says Campbell,

---

[73] Lord Raglan, *The Hero: A Study in Tradition, Myth, and Drama* (New York, 1956), 183-84.

[74] Nennius mentions it in explanation of the origin of the name of Carn Cabal given to a heap of stones. Loomis describes this story and says that this cairn still gives its name to a heap of stones in northern Breconshire (*Arthurian Tradition*, pp. 12-13).

[75] Entry *Twrch Trwyth*, in Gertrude Jobes, *Dictionary of Mythology, Folklore, and Symbols* (New York, 1961).

is a personage of exceptional gifts. Frequently he is honored by his society, frequently unrecognized or disdained. He and/or the world in which he finds himself suffers from a symbological deficiency. In fairy tales this may be as slight as the lack of a certain golden ring, whereas in apocalyptic vision the physical and spiritual life of the whole earth can be represented as fallen, or on the point of falling, into ruin. Typically, the hero of the fairy tale achieves a domestic, microcosmic triumph, and the hero of myth a world-historical, macrocosmic triumph. Whereas the former... prevails over his personal oppressors, the latter brings back from his adventure the means for the regeneration of his society as a whole. [76]

These contrasted patterns of fairy-hero and monomyth-hero explain in part the confusion which has arisen from the consideration of *Guingamor* as a lay of the usual fairy-mistress type. In *Guingamor* the advances of the queen to the young knight make him aware of a serious failing in the beautiful courtly world ruled by his uncle. It is the presence of lechery, of *luxuria*. He leaves the court in response to the queen's veiled challenge, to prove himself master of the boar which symbolizes that which he had refused to accept in the queen and which forms the concealed weakness. [77]

And what of the lay's ending? Here again the hero monomyth affords valuable suggestions. We recall that *Lanval* and *Graelent*, tales which are comparable to *Guingamor* in so many elements of the *matière*, end happily, with the knights being absolved of suspicion before the society which is their frame of reference and triumphantly reinstated into the favor of the fairy *amie*. This is not the sort of triumph which Guingamor expects as the reward for his success. He is eager, even while enjoying the company of

---

[76] *Op. cit.*, pp. 37-38.
[77] In the poem, then, Guingamor responds to a challenge arising from a flaw in the courtly society, not directly in himself. An interesting parallel is furnished by *Sir Gawain and the Green Knight*, in which, as Moorman points out, the failure of a whole social order is implicit. "Morgan's testing of Gawain is designed to warn the court of two potential dangers, sexual wantonness and unfaithfulness. Wantonness is personified by Guinevere, who, we remember, is later to bring about the downfall of the court by her affair with Lancelot" (*op. cit.*, p. 68).

the fay (which Lanval and Graelent are busily sacrificing all else in order to enjoy), to return to his uncle's court with the boar's head which is the token of his victory, and with the account of his *aventure*. If he is but a callow youth interested in boasting about his virility, as Damon suggests,[78] the tale is of course one which may be fitted readily into the fairy-mistress category, although even in this case some of its deviations from the type are difficult to account for; however, if he is a quester after something dangerous and deeply significant, if his hunt is in fact an attempt to vanquish *luxuria*, then it is entirely consistent with the main focus of the poem for him to insist on returning as quickly as possible to the society whose weakness caused him to set out on the quest, and to present to that society the head of the boar.

In connection with the monomyth and its application to this poem, the comments by Cirlot on the symbolism of knighthood itself are most interesting. The cult of the hero developed, says Cirlot, "because of the virtues inherent in heroism —virtues which have surely been apparent to Man from prehistoric times and which he has felt the need to exalt, emphasize, and record... Every heroic characteristic has its analogy among the virtues necessary to vanquish chaos and overcome the temptations offered by the forces of darkness... The first object of the hero is to conquer himself."[79] Moorman in his study of the knight in literature discusses the strong case "for the theory that the varying forms of the journey motif may be manifestations of a single, extended metaphor involving the recreation, in literary terms, of the quest myth, the *rite de passage*, Toynbee's withdrawal and return (any number of terms will do), the ritual journey marking the transition from youthful innocence and ignorance to self knowledge, maturity, and, in religious terms, salvation."[80] Cirlot extends his discussion of the hero with a most significant comment: "A hero turned Christian is a hero turned knight."[81] Knighthood is to be seen as "a superior kind of pedagogy helping

---

[78] *Op. cit.*, p. 987.
[79] *Op. cit.*, p. 140.
[80] *Op. cit.*, p. 3.
[81] *Op. cit.*, p. 141.

to bring about the transmutation of natural man (steedless) into spiritual man. An important part was played in the symbolic tradition by prototypes such as the famous mythical knights of the court of King Arthur, or patron saints such as St. George, Santiago of Compostela, or the Archangel Michael. The practical means of achieving the knight's goal consisted of corporal exertions, which were, in effect, not merely physical or material..." [82] Exertions of this sort made an apprenticeship, then, which "led eventually to the inversion of the world of desire through the ascetic denial of physical pleasure," and in this sense too the knight-errant is to be interpreted as striving to master his desires. [83]

Knighthood thus may be seen in one of its aspects as a struggle to achieve the triumph of morality and of the spiritual nature of man. Furthermore, as Moorman points out, a moral problem is inherent in the concept of knighthood itself, for "the historical concept of chivalry presented the knight with a contradictory code of ethics," so that the truly great works on the theme of chivalry consider the inevitable moral dilemmas encountered by the knight. [84] "From the eleventh through the fifteenth centuries, chivalry was in varying degrees an operative mode of life, an ethic, and the myth of the questing hero the natural means of its expression... there is present a sense of urgency, no mere use of the knight as a literary device but a concern for the morality of knighthood itself." [85]

If the results of this study are correct, *Guingamor* is not simply another *remaniement* of a prototype fairy-mistress tale. Its anonymous poet was not borrowing at random from various traditions, combining disparate elements and failing to achieve their fusion into a coherent whole. The lay appears, in the light of the proposed interpretation, as a complex poem in which each element is carefully fitted into an overall conception. The questions left unanswered by scholars have all been based on considerations of the lay as representative of one or more traditions, whereas the poet was interested in the traditions only as they

---

[82] *Ibid.*, pp. 162-63.
[83] *Ibid.*, p. 164.
[84] *Op. cit.*, p. 7.
[85] *Ibid.*, p. 151.

furnished him with a framework of certain interest which he could modify to his own demands. The Potiphar's-wife episode would not be a good induction to a fairy-mistress tale, but it is a very appropriate induction to a quest related to moral strength or weakness. The boar would be a poor attempt at disguising the poet's extensive borrowing from other tales, but it is a very appropriate symbol for the *luxuria* exemplified by the queen's behavior. The fay who becomes Guingamor's *amie* acts in a way which would be very odd for a mere fairy mistress, but which is entirely appropriate for a representative of the spirit's higher powers aiding the hero against its lower powers as embodied in the boar. The position and function of the apple incident at the lay's conclusion would be evidence of ineptitude in handling traditional fairy-mistress and Otherworld-voyage material, but they are in fact evidence of the poet's skill in combining disparate elements into a remarkably coherent symbolic whole to which that traditional material is relevant only as framework. In other words, as a fairy-mistress and Otherworld-voyage tale the lay of *Guingamor* is indeed incoherent; but as a symbolic representation of the struggle by a hero to overcome the forces of moral degradation it is both an artistic success and a good example of the medieval ability to use traditional *matière* as the vehicle for profound *sens*.[86]

There are two basic objections which are likely to be raised against such an interpretation: that its terms are moral and Christian, when we have before us a mere fairy story or at most a combination of fairy-mistress and Otherworld-voyage traditions; and that it is symbolic, while such tales were designed merely to entertain. These objections cannot be met absolutely, as no evidence in a literary work is of an absolute kind. The first objection, however, may be answered with the reminder that fairy

---

[86] It is interesting to note that W. P. Ker considers *Guingamor* a leading example of the earliest type of romances, which in his opinion were "generally content if they could get the matter in the right order and present it in simple language, like tunes played with one finger. One great advantage of this procedure is that the stories are intelligible." In *Guingamor* "the story is allowed to account for the full value of all its incidents, with scarcely a touch to heighten the importance of any of them. It is the argument of a story, and little more" (*op. cit.*, pp. 337-38).

tales, just as tales of classical antiquity, were subject to Christian and moral interpretations, and that in any case we do not have here a mere fairy story, but rather a combination of elements, some of them traditional, to form something wholly new.

It is precisely the consideration of *Guingamor* in terms of its traditions exclusively that has led critics to abandon the attempt to explain certain of its elements. H. Newstead termed *Guingamor* "a fairy mistress tale difficult to bring into the Christian orbit," [87] while in fact the poem does not require to be brought into that orbit, having most likely originated there; it is rather the fairy-mistress elements which must be explained in terms of their contribution to the lay's basic conception.

To meet the second objection, we may refer to the evidence which modern scholarship is gradually providing that the medieval interest in fairy tales was not due exclusively and necessarily to the appeal of a pretty story. The lays, like the romances, were serious literary efforts, and as Holmes and Klenke emphasize, "an inner sense is always present in any serious production of the Middle Ages." [88] We are beginning to realize that the prevalence of symbolic and mythical interpretation in the medieval period was considerably greater than many scholars have been willing to admit, particularly with regard to literature. [89] D. W. Robertson, Jr. asserts the doctrine of charity as a dominant theme in

---

[87] *Bran the Blessed*, p. 126.
[88] *Op. cit.*, v. Resistance to such interpretation has, however, been strong. "In recent years the Christian, Celtic, and ritualistic explanations have been obliged to contend with a negative approach which has been increasing. Certain scholars have renounced all claim to explain the pattern of detail introduced by Chrétien into the Grail Quest and the Gawain adventures. Those who accept this viewpoint abandon all attempt to study the *sens*; they accept the *matière* alone. When *sens* is explained it is made to seem very trivial" (Holmes and Klenke, vi). This resistance is frequently even stronger with regard to works less thoroughly studied than those of Chrétien or of Marie.
[89] See, for example, Morton W. Bloomfield, "Symbolism in Medieval Literature," *MP*, LVI, 73-81; D. W. Robertson, Jr., "Some Medieval Literary Terminology with Special Reference to Chrétien de Troyes," *SP*, XLVIII (1951), 669-92; Leo Spitzer, "The Prologue to the *Lais* of Marie de France and Medieval Poetics," *MP*, XLI (1943), 96-102. See also, for interpretations of medieval works and an attempted synthesis, the papers in *Critical Approaches to Medieval Literature: Selected Papers from the English Institute, 1958-1959* (New York, 1960).

medieval literature, and cites a number of examples of the Fathers of the Church encouraging symbolic interpretation, with Augustine leading the way: "Nos quid quid illud signicat faciamus et quam sit verum non laboremus." [90]

Profane letters as well as the Bible were considered as allegorical. Bezzola asserts that with the Carolingian renaissance "la science religieuse et la science profane (*les artes*) sont réunies en un édifice qui embrasse toutes les connaissances humaines," and adds a justification for his own symbolic interpretation of events in the *Erec*: "Comment admettre que, dans ce monde habitué à sonner à chaque chose et à chaque attitude un sens plus profond, la littérature narrative profane et en particulier le roman courtois se soient bornés à raconter des faits, des aventures n'exprimant que ce qu'implique leur sens littéral?" [91] A. Béguin emphasizes the necessity of symbolic interpretation in his preface to Bezzola's work, stating that in medieval conceptions "toute la réalité sensible est composée de symboles et demande à être sans cesse traduite ...Le moyen âge voit à la fois, d'un même regard, la chose et son sens, l'objet sensible et ce qui est au-delà du sensible, le geste humain et sa valeur de rite, les couleurs et leur correspondance secrète dans le domaine de l'âme." [92] Spitzer has discussed medieval narratives in terms of a "logique symbolique," [93] and Jodogne replied to the doubts which Pierre le Gentil expressed about Spitzer's critical principles with the comment that "le risque d'erreur dans la résolution des symboles serait moins grave que le dédain des menus détails, couleurs, éléments de la faune et de la flore, dont les virtualités symboliques étaient connues des clercs, commes celles du livre d'Isaïe, et considérées par la philosophie réaliste comme les rudiments de la vraie science." [94] We should note also that literary scholarship has not been alone in producing this new appreciation of a significant aspect of medieval literature.

---

[90] "The Doctrine of Charity," pp. 24ff. Cirlot, T. H. White, and a number of others have pointed out the importance of Augustine's encouragement of symbolic interpretation.

[91] *Op. cit.*, p. 7.

[92] In *ibid.*, Préface, v.

[93] Discussed in O. Jodogne, "L'interprétation des textes médiévaux," *Lettres romanes*, VIII (1953), 369-70.

[94] *Ibid.*, p. 370.

One of the most influential commentors on this topic has been Jung, who observes concerning the intimate nature of medieval symbolism that in those days "analogy was not so much a logical figure as a secret identity." [95]

Perhaps the most direct expression of this tendency to symbolism in medieval works is that of T. H. White, who states that a symbol "is a metaphor, a parable, a parallelism, a part of a pattern," [96] and points out that the most disparate elements might be united readily by the medieval mind on the basis of a pattern linkage. It is such a link in pattern that we have been investigating in *Guingamor*, and we have found that the traditional fairy-mistress and Otherworld-voyage tales, which contribute to the lay's *matière*, provide patterns which are suggestive of moral and Christian elements. These moral and Christian elements form the underlying pattern of *Guingamor*, a pattern determining the detail of the form assumed by the traditional material of the narrative.

---

[95] Quoted in Cirlot, xxii.
[96] T. H. White, trsl. and ed., *The Bestiary: A Book of Beasts* (New York, 1960), 244.

BIBLIOGRAPHY

ANWYL, E. "Arthur, Arthurian Cycle," *Encyclopaedia of Religion and Ethics*, ed. J. Hastings, II, 1-7.
BEZZOLA, R. R. *Le sens de l'aventure et de l'amour (Chrétien de Troyes)*. Paris, 1947.
BLOOMFIELD, M. "Symbolism in Medieval Literature," *Modern Philology*, LVI (1956), 73-81.
BODKIN, MAUD. *Archetypal Patterns in Poetry: Psychological Studies of Imagination*. London, 1963.
BOETHIUS. *The Consolation of Philosophy*, trsl. J. J. Buchanan. New York, 1957.
BROWN, A. C. L. "A Note on the *Nugae* of G. H. Gerould's 'King Arthur and Politics'," *Speculum*, II (1927), 449-455.
———. "From Cauldron of Plenty to Grail," *Modern Philology*, XIV (1916), 385-404.
———. "The Wonderful Flower that Came to St. Brendan," *Manly Anniversary Studies* (Chicago, 1923), 296-297.
BRUGGER, E. "Eigennamen in den Lais der Marie de France," *Zeitschrift für französische Sprache und Literatur*, XLIX (1927), 201-252.
CAMPBELL, JOSEPH. *The Hero with a Thousand Faces*. Cleveland and New York, 1966.
CHAMBERS, E. K. *Arthur of Britain*. London, 1927.
CIRLOT, J. E. *A Dictionary of Symbols*, translated from the Spanish by Jack Sage. New York, 1962.
CONS, LOUIS. "Avallo," *Modern Philology*, XXVIII (1931), 385-394.
Critical Approaches to Medieval Literature: Selected Papers from the English Institute, 1958-1959. New York, 1960.
CROSS, T. P. "The Celtic Elements in the Lays of *Lanval* and *Graelent*," *Modern Philology*, XII, no. 10 (1915), 585-644.
———. "The Celtic 'Fée' in 'Launfal'," *Kittredge Anniversary Papers* (Boston, 1923), 377-387.
———. "The Passing of Arthur," *Manly Anniversary Studies* (Chicago, 1923), 284-294.
CURTIN, J. *Myths and Folk-Lore of Ireland*. Boston, 1890.
DAMON, S. FOSTER. "Marie de France — Psychologist of Courtly Love," *PMLA*, XLIV (1929), 968-996.
DRUCE, G. C. "The Sow and Pigs; A Study in Metaphor," *Archaeologia Cantiana*, XLVI, 1-6.
EWERT, A., ed. *Marie de France, Lais*. Oxford, 1963.

FARAL, E. "L'Ile d'Avallon et la Fée Morgane," *Mélanges Jeanroy* (Paris, 1928), 243-253.
———. *La Légende Arthurienne, Etudes et Documents*. 3 vols. Paris, 1929.
FAVERTY, F. E. "The Story of Joseph and Potiphar's Wife in Medieval Literature," (*Harvard*) *Studies and Notes in Philology and Literature*, XIII (1931), 81-127.
FERGUSON, GEORGE. *Signs and Symbols in Christian Art*. New York, 1961.
FREYMOND, E. "Beitrage zur Kenntnis der altfranzösische Artus-romane in Prosa," *Zeitschrift für französische Sprache und Literatur*, XVII (1895), 1-128.
HARTLAND, E. S. *The Science of Fairy Tales*. New York, 1891.
HOEPFFNER, E. "Graëlent ou Lanval?" *Recueil de travaux offert à M. C. Brunel* (Paris, 1955), 1-8.
———. "Marie de France et les Lais Anonymes," *Studi Medievali*, N. S. 4 (1931), 1-31.
HOFER, S. "Kritische Bemerkungen zum Lai de Guingamor," *Romanische Forschungen*, LXV (1954), 360-377.
HOLBROOK, R. T. *Dante and the Animal Kingdom*. New York, 1966.
HOLMES, URBAN T., Jr. and Sister M. Amelia Klenke, O. P. *Chrétien, Troyes, and the Grail*. Chapel Hill, 1959.
INMAN, T. *Ancient Pagan and Modern Christian Symbolism*. New York, 1875.
JOBES, GERTRUDE. *Dictionary of Mythology, Folklore and Symbols*. New York, 1961.
JODOGNE, O. "L'interprétation des textes médiévaux," *Lettres romanes*, VII (1953), 369-370.
KEIGHTLEY, T. *Fairy Mythology*. London, 1889.
KER, W. P. *Epic and Romance*. London, 1908.
KITTREDGE, G. L. *A Study of Gawain and the Green Knight*. Cambridge, Mass., 1916.
KRAPPE, A. H. *La Genèse des Mythes*. Paris, 1938.
LOOMIS, C. GRANT. *White Magic: An Introduction to the Folklore of Christian Legend*. Cambridge, Mass., 1948.
LOOMIS, R. S. *Arthurian Tradition and Chrétien de Troyes*. New York, 1949.
———. "Arthurian Tradition and Folklore," *Folklore*, LXIX (1958), 1-25.
———. *Celtic Myth and Arthurian Romance*. New York, 1927.
———. "A Survey of Scholarship on the Fairy Mythology of Arthurian Romance since 1903" in L. Paton, *Studies in the Fairy Mythology of Arthurian Romance*, 2nd ed. New York, 1960, 280-307.
———. "Etudes sur la provenance du cycle arthurien," *Romania*, XXIV (1895), 497-528.
———. "Nouveaux Essais sur la Provenance du Cycle Arthurien," *Romania*, XXVIII (1899), 1-48 and 321-328.
———. "Nouvelles Etudes sur la Provenance du Cycle Arthurien," *Romania*, XXVII (1898), 527-573.
———. "Nouvelles Etudes sur la Provenance du Cycle Arthurien," *Romania*, XXX (1901), 1-10.
LOTH, J., ed. *Les Mabinogion*. Paris, 1913.
———. "Des nouvelles théories sur l'origine des romans Arthuriens," *Revue celtique* (1892), 475-503.

MACCULLOCH, J. A. "Blest, Abode of the (Celtic)," *Encyclopaedia of Religion and Ethics*, ed. J. Hastings, II, 689-696.
———. "Fairy," *Encyclopaedia of Religion and Ethics*, ed. J. Hastings, V, 678-689.
MAURY, A. *Croyances et Légendes du Moyen Age*. Paris, 1896.
MEYER, KUNO, ed. *The Voyage of Bran*. 2 vols. London, 1895.
MOORMAN, C. *A Knyght There Was: The Evolution of the Knight in Literature*. Lexington, 1967.
———. "Myth and Medieval Literature: *Sir Gawain and the Green Knight*," *Mediaeval Studies*, XVIII (1956), 158-172.
NEWSTEAD, H. *Bran the Blessed in Arthurian Romance*. New York, 1939.
———. "The Traditional Background of *Partonopeus de Blois*," *PMLA*, LXI (1946), 916-946.
———. "Yvain and the Myth of the Fountain," *Speculum*, XXX (1955), 170-179.
NUTT, A. "The Happy Otherworld in the Mythico-Romantic Literature of the Irish," *The Voyage of Bran*, ed. Kuno Meyer. London, 1895.
PARIS, G. "Caradoc et le Serpent," *Romania*, XXVIII (1899), 214-231.
———. "Lais inédits de Tyolet, de Guingamor, de Doon, du Lecheor et de Tydorel," *Romania*, VIII (1879), 29-72.
Partonopeus de Blois, ed. A. C. M. Robert. Paris, 1834.
PATCH, H. R. *The Other World, according to descriptions in medieval literature*. Cambridge, Mass., 1950.
PATON, LUCY. *Studies in the Fairy Mythology of Arthurian Romance*. 2nd edition, with a survey of scholarship since 1903 and a bibliography by R. S. Loomis. New York, 1960.
PÉPIN, J. *Mythe et Allégorie*. Paris, 1958.
PHILIPOT, E. "Un Episode d'Erec et Enide," *Romania*, XXV (1896), 259-294.
RAGLAN, LORD. *The Hero: A Study in Tradition, Myth, and Drama*. New York, 1956.
REINHARD, J. R., *The Survival of Geis in Medieval Romance*. Halle, 1933.
RHYS, J. *Celtic Folklore, Welsh and Manx*. Oxford, 1901.
———. *Studies in the Arthurian Legend*. Oxford, 1891.
"Rigomer," *Histoire littéraire de la France*, XXX, 93.
ROBERTSON, D. W. JR. "The Doctrine of Charity in Medieval Literary Gardens," *Speculum*, XXVI (1951), 24-49.
———. "Some Medieval Literary Terminology with Special Reference to Chrétien de Troyes," *Studies in Philology*, XLVIII (1951), 669-692.
SAVAGE, HENRY L. "The Significance of the Hunting Scenes in *Gawain and the Green Knight*," *Journal of English and Germanic Philology*, XXVII (1928), 1-15.
SCHOFIELD, W. H. "The Lay of Guingamor," *(Harvard) Studies and Notes in Philology and Literature*, V (1896), 221-243.
———. "The Lays of Graelent and Lanval and the Story of Wayland," *PMLA*, XV (1900), 121-180.
SEGRE, C. "Lanval, Graëlent, Guingamor," *Studi in onore de Angelo Monteverdi*, II (Modena, 1959), 756-770.
SLOVER, C. H. "Avalon," *Modern Philology*, XXVIII (1931), 395-399.
SPITZER, L. "The Prologue to the Lais of Marie de France and Medieval Poetics," *Modern Philology*, XLI (1943), 96-102.
WARREN, F. M. "Avalon," *Modern Language Notes*, XIV (1899), 94-95.

WHITE, T. H., trsl. and ed. *The Bestiary: A Book of Beasts*. New York, 1960.
WILLIAMS, G. PERRIE, ed. *Le Bel Inconnu*. Paris, 1929 (CFMA).
WILLIAMS, H. F. "The Anonymous Breton Lays," *Research Studies*, XXXII (1964), 76-84.
WOODS, WILLIAM S. "The Plot Structure in Four Romances of Chrétien de Troyes," *Studies in Philology*, L (1953), 4-15.
ZIMMER, H. "Beiträge zur Namenforschung in den altfranzösische Arthurepen," *Zeitschrift für französische Sprache und Literatur*, XIII, i (1891), 1-117.

www.ingramcontent.com/pod-product-compliance
Lightning Source LLC
Chambersburg PA
CBHW020420230426
43663CB00007BA/1251